T0194844

Praise for *How I Met My Guardian Angel*

Robbie H. Andrews's personal story will resonate with many readers who have at one time felt lost. I found it to be a compelling read; I could hardly put it down. It offers the reader hope, and delivers wisdom that will light the path for many.

Dr. David R. Hamilton,
Hay House Author of Is Your Life Mapped Out?

Robbie's book is a hugely engaging read, but it is so much more than that too. It's evidence of the wondrous relationship we can all have with the angelic realm, if we simply open ourselves up to it.

Robbie writes from the heart and soul with honesty and passion. This is a must read for anyone wanting to progress along their spiritual path and deepen their connection with the angels.

Tracie Couper,
features editor of Spirit & Destiny Magazine

It's a long time since I was given an angel book that was so readable, so down to earth, and presented with such honesty and humility.

Written retrospectively, having awakened to his true soul purpose and the divine gifts of healing and clear-sight; having experienced so many life affirming spiritual phenomena, as well as the ecstatic highs and soul wrenching lows of a troubled journey ... this book comes straight from the heart.

It expresses part of a young man's life story; full of the drama and self-indulgence of escapism, the emotional suffering, love and pain that is so often experienced by someone suppressing their spirituality and true life purpose, and takes us to an amazing and beautiful realization and outcome.

Robbie's wonderfully Irish, page turning story-telling style bravely reveals a deep vulnerability which actually moved me to tears at times, spontaneously laughing out loud at others.

My favorite part of the book, not surprisingly, were the angelic encounters with Robbie's guardian angel which for me brought tears of pure joy and connection. The sheer clarity, depth and beauty of these words of wisdom, given by Robbie's angels to share with other seekers on the road ahead, really are divinely inspired. There is no doubt that the angels words, through Robbie's reflection, will echo with a resonance that will make the hairs on your neck stand on end. As you read them, and they speak to your heart, they will call to your soul, and remind you ... that faith, hope and love are truly all that matters.

Chrissie Astell, best-selling
spiritual author

Reading Robbie's book was a Kaleidoscope of wild and wonderful adventures. I could not put his book down. Robbie reveals himself to be a true warrior. This is a story full of shocking experiences.

A memoir of catastrophic timeline events in history based in New York, that propels you straight to the scene of time and place. A heart pumping story, soul-aching, full of pain and triumph! I cried my eyes out reading the book, it was so rich in exploring my own feelings about trusting *God's Plan*. It was as if the book mirrored my past life experiences, feelings and emotions. I absolutely loved Robbie's courageous story. A true story of one man's strength and bravery, with a beautiful message of Hope that will reach the hearts and minds of many. God has a plan for us all and *How I Met My Guardian Angel* is an easy-to-read page turner. Left me wanting to know more. Looking forward to reading the second part of the book.

Judith L. May
Managing Director, Quantum Biomed Farms Ireland

How I Met My
Guardian Angel

From Madness to Meditation Trilogy

BOOK ONE

Robbie H. Andrews

BALBOA.PRESS
A DIVISION OF HAY HOUSE

Balboa Press books may be ordered through booksellers or by contacting:

Balboa Press
A Division of Hay House
1663 Liberty Drive
Bloomington, IN 47403
www.balboapress.com
844-682-1282

Scripture quotations marked KJV are from the Holy Bible, King James Version (Authorized Version). First published in 1611. Quoted from the KJV Classic Reference Bible, Copyright © 1983 by The Zondervan Corporation.

Unless otherwise indicated, all scripture quotations are from The Holy Bible, English Standard Version® (ESV®). Copyright ©2001 by Crossway Bibles, a division of Good News Publishers. Used by permission. All rights reserved.

Print information available on the last page.

ISBN: 978-1-9822-5946-4 (sc)
ISBN: 978-1-9822-5947-1 (hc)
ISBN: 978-1-9822-5945-7 (e)

Library of Congress Control Number: 2020923342

Balboa Press rev. date: 12/14/2020

I dedicate this book to you, the reader.
Love, love, always love.

In the beginning was the word,
and the word was with God,
and the word was God.
(John 1:1 KJV)

Contents

Preface

My Story

I'm alive, I'm awake, and I'm living in the knowing of my own truth.

Since the day I met my guardian angel—when she brought me the beautiful validation of love, faith, and hope—my life has changed in more ways than I could have ever imagined. As I get this opportunity to share my journey with you, from the depths of darkness to the greatest light of all, I feel truly honored. I've held onto my truth.

Your time will come.

I've sat patiently for many years, meditating and waiting for that sign from God and his angels. I was waiting to receive that all-important message.

The time is now.

As I share my story, I ask, what can I tell you that would help you? How can I share the knowledge I've learned to help you overcome the many obstacles in your path? From darkness and depression to anguish and pain and suffering, life takes no prisoners.

You have a purpose in your life, and the light of God is only a thought away.

This story begins in my early twenties and spans three years of my life. There are many more years to be covered, but for now I will take you back through some events in my life to give you an understanding of how and why I'm here. In the depths of my darkness, I found a glimmer of light that would eventually bring me back to a place that had meaning.

Only through my darkness could I find my light and from this, from the depths of the soul, I began to heal.

I would have to make my way through the patterns of past and future thinking to get to the present moment. I was exploring the feeling of being lonely, and I was crying for help. I just wanted someone to understand how I felt. Why did I have so many questions but could not find the answers? Finding them was all part of the journey I would have to endure.

Why has God abandoned me? Why is this world so unreal to me? Who writes the rules we're living under?

Why do I feel God is something that exists outside of me?

It was like there was a separation between God and me. It felt like we were two different things—separate entities. It was like the God I was taught about belonged in a book, and this never felt right for me. I struggled to connect to those teachings. I found myself moving away from God, yet on the other hand, somewhere deep in my being, I longed to find out what I really felt within my soul.

I asked myself, *Does God really sit on a throne?* I remembered the words that I had heard so many times in my life—that we are all children of God and that the love God has for us knows no bounds.

But I just couldn't connect to this God, in a book or on a throne, because somewhere within, I felt disconnected and out of harmony. I felt like there had to be more to this life, but what if there wasn't? I had this ongoing battle, struggling to find validation and truth in my life.

In this world of emotions, I had no way of expressing what was going on internally. I felt like I was being misled, trying to discover something I saw no value in.

Why does this place have to be so hard?

I have so much to share, but I want you to understand that while meeting my guardian angel was a blessing, God is the pinnacle of all you should seek. I hope that my story is one that will help you to open your eyes, heart, and mind. We can all change and grow, and we can all become so aware. There is no emotion that we cannot conquer through the great powers of wisdom and experience. We have to walk in our own truth and self-belief, and not in that of others.

Remembering who we are is important.

We have mislaid our truth of who we really are and what we are capable of. Modern life and forms of media have formed so many false realities and concepts. These outlets portray only what they want you to see and only guide you to lands they want you to explore. But what if there is much more beyond them? What if you start seeing things through your own eyes, for no one else but you?

To do this—to find your answers—it's important that you understand our world and your emotions. This is a time on our earth in which we are urged to take down the barriers that have surrounded us for many lifetimes, to break through the illusion of delusion and really see our true power. This is the essence of who we are and what lies within.

It's crucial to know your essence, from which you came: the grace of God, the source that is within us all. You are the creator of your thoughts and actions, and you carry the karmic responsibility of this. Can you accept this part of who you are? Can you handle your inner power and take back the control from other forces—from the darkness and from all that is born there? Are you afraid of this? Are you afraid of being empowered and using it for pure goodness?

For a long time now, people have been disempowered so that others could be in control. Religions told you that God was to be feared and was outside of you, a separate being of power. But I know that this is not true, for every soul has an equal God within them, and no one soul is more special than any other on this earth. When searching for God, stop searching externally. He rules in the deepest, brightest parts of your internal capacity.

You and you alone, are the one who leads by your example. It is time to walk your way out of the veil of illusion and into the light that you are. My message to you is one of hope, sent to me by God through the presence of my guardian angel.

Within the pages of this book, I will explain this meaning and will reveal to you the ways in which I have discovered my answers. Come along and join me on my journey, for your own answers may be closer than you think.

Acknowledgments

This is the part of the book where I get to give a heartfelt thank you to everyone who has helped me along the way. So many people have been involved in my journey, so if I do happen to miss a few, please forgive me and consider this to be your honorable mention. Thank you.

I want to start off by saying a massive thank you to my beautiful girlfriend, Lynn, and our daughter Ariah. This book has created a landslide of emotions, and finding it in me to begin again has not been easy. However, without Lynn, it would have been a whole lot harder. I also want to give a very special mention to my daughter, Bella-May. I love you.

Thanks to my mother, Jacinta, and my father, Henry, whom I love dearly. Thanks to my brother, Joe, my sister, Vicky, and my little brother, Jason. Thank you for standing behind me through all the tough times; what a journey it's been. I love you all.

Vicky, I will never be able to fully communicate the gratitude I hold deep in my heart. Thanks for being there when I needed you most.

I want to thank Jason's girlfriend, Katie—aka Lola Liner. I'm super proud of you. Keep following your dreams.

Thanks to my brother-in-law, Nick. Big thanks to all my nephews and nieces: Emmet, Cian, Teagan, James, David, and Sophie.

Thank you to my late grandparents: Harry and Sarah Andrews and Paddy and Nancy Walsh. I've been very lucky to have you all and to have you by my side and alive for most of my life.

Nanna Walsh, you have been such an inspiration to me in this life. I have learned so much from your love and wisdom. I will be eternally grateful for every moment we have shared. You mean the world to me. I love you.

Grandad Paddy, you live in my heart always. You were such a huge part of my life. Your influence on this story changed so much for me. I can't wait until our time comes to meet again.

A massive thank you goes to Uncle Brian and Aunt Tammy. You were the hand that reached out and pulled me toward God's light during a very dark time in my life. You helped me to see and feel the bridges I needed to cross to get me on the path to where I am now.

Thanks to Neala McPhail for making that phone call from America and for being a friend forever.

To my aunt and uncle, Ann and Paul Henry, thank you for being there for me.

Thank you to Sandra Poland Barry for the beautiful poem, "The Sign." This will always be a special part of the book to me.

Thanks to my very good friend Stephen "Spock" Geraghty, his partner, Lisa, and their daughter, Summer. I am so grateful for your support.

I would also like to thank Jon-Paul Donnelly (JP) and my close friend Nicky Archer. We might not see one another day after day, but whenever we do meet up, it's like we never parted.

I want to give a special thanks to my very close friend Frances Bolger Kiely. For the short time we've been friends, you have been there for me regardless, and from the start, I knew we were meant to be friends for many lifetimes.

To my friend John McEnaney, thank you. Special thanks also to Dave Viney.

To all the people who, for one reason or another, have been a part of my life, I extend to you my heartfelt gratitude and love. Thanks to the following wonderful people who have so kindly reviewed my book: Dr. David Hamilton, Dr. Kyl Smith, Chrissie Astell, Tracie Couper, and Judith L. May.

My last thank you goes to Des. God put you into my life at a time when I needed help, I am grateful beyond words.

1

Every Beginning Has a Story

I was living in a small town in Ireland called Drogheda. I was so lost, with no understanding of my purpose or what it meant to be living a full life; I felt I was stuck on a conveyor belt. During this period, I, like many other young people, was living a life with very little meaning. I was in a dream world, out of touch with myself, living life in a bubble, thinking and feeling that I was invincible or bulletproof—that the world owed me something. Yet somewhere deep inside, I knew I wanted to find my place in the world. This process would involve my taking a few knocks and bangs because that's what it would take to open my eyes!

As a child I seemed to float unnoticed, beneath the radar of school and the educational system, and for the most part I was left to my own misunderstood devices. I was a right-brain thinker, so the left brain of logical education was foreign to me. As I couldn't really connect with it, I switched it off, in a way. That left me with a lack of communication skills because I had no one to guide me or teach me in a way that was needed. Writing English became a problem for me, but the adults seemed to be okay with letting me drift along—and I sure was okay with that at the time. I can see this now, but at the time I had no clue what was happening.

My adolescence mostly consisted of recreational drug use and partying the weekends away as a form of escapism. That was the in thing in my town; you weren't a nineties kid in Ireland if you weren't doing that. I was living a double life—happy on the outside but in so much pain on the inside, trying to understand the duality of this world. I was living a life that couldn't have been further from my truth. I had no understanding and didn't know who could help me. What am I saying? I didn't even think I needed help!

I always felt like I slipped under the radar. However, contradictory as it may sound, somewhere in my being I was aware that something was missing and that my truth would look for me.

I was always very different. I felt this as a child, and the feeling lingered long into my teens. How differently my life would turn out would not be fully exposed until my early twenties. During the time leading to this, I felt like two different people. There was the kind child Robbie, who wanted to be loved and not feel lost, hurt, or angry. Then there was what I portrayed to the world: a Jack the Lad, never in trouble but finding myself in and around trouble without really understanding why. I was hurting and found myself around people who were also hurting.

Taking drugs was definitely a form of escapism. I started experimenting with drugs in my teenage years, just like a lot of other young people around me. I had come through so many experiences up until that point. It seemed to be the way to go, always hiding from one aspect of my life. To others, I was the one who was leading the way. Drugs were my release; they became my escape. When I look back now, I can see where God, and his angels were there to help me. They have truly never failed me throughout my journey—I just couldn't see that until the day I met my guardian angel.

My childhood was an explosive one, with lots of different hurts and pains. I grew up with two brothers and one sister. I am the second eldest; there is also my older brother, Joe, younger sister, Vickie, and the baby of the family, Jason. My parents were hardworking. Henry, my dad, worked in a factory and drove a taxi, while my mom, Jacinta, worked in a factory as a cleaner. She was very proud of her skills both in keeping house and as a mother. Growing up in my family wasn't an easy process, as there always seemed to be some sort of hurt or pain for me. I never could understand why there was so much tension in my family home and why we as a family unit often got into heated arguments. The answers regarding my childhood and the things I experienced would not come to me until God sent my guardian angel into my life.

I was really intuitive as a child, but at the time I blocked this awareness due to my experiences, and that led me to the opposite end of the scale: skepticism.

My childhood was such a tough place for me to visit in my heart and mind, and part of me was hiding the hurt and pain from my experiences. I had been trying so hard for the most of my life to understand why I felt so disconnected from God and from my parents. The love I felt inside of me was not what I was experiencing in my world. Love was not always openly expressed in our family, so it didn't provide an outlet for me. I didn't hear the words, "I love you." Finding the answers and the soul that is within would take me on a journey I could never have foreseen. When my guardian angel came to me, I was at a point in my life where I had lost all faith. I was feeling so damaged—this is when my guardian angel led me back to God and into a place of harmony.

Only through my darkness could I find my light.

We as humans feel so many different emotions, and how we use them can determine the paths we take. We all know that the wind can blow on our faces one moment, yet the next we can't find a breath and feel like we're suffocating, like our lives are slipping away. Has anyone ever told you that it's okay just to be you?

We have all felt many emotions through our misguided understanding of life; the rights and wrongs of people's judgements project on our journeys. Some are positive. But in my case, most were not.

I am here to help all who encounter me in this lifetime to really see their true light and their value and to understand that it's time to take charge and start to live life in a way that has complete meaning. You *will* find the strength and courage to take you through this day and the next. I know this because my guardian angel told me exactly that and helped me believe it too. This is the reason I can now help others. It's not that I am wiser than you; it's just that I have been through the darkness yet still emerged on the other side and moved into the light.

Lean on me, for I am standing tall today. My light will bring you through the perils of your darkness and let you see how bright you shine. Lights shine to guide the way, not to take the light away from others.

Hope—it's in hope that we will find ourselves.

In October 2000, my grandfather passed away after a battle with cancer. He was only properly diagnosed two weeks beforehand. Toward the end of his life, our family experienced a great deal of pain. This was especially the case for my mom. In my grandfather's home, family life was precious. My mom's family was a large, traditional Irish family that consisted of nine boys and five girls. Watching my grandfather fade away so fast was immensely painful for every single one of them. I loved him so much. We all did, and I didn't understand how the world could be so cruel, how it could have him taken away in a great deal of pain and so quickly. The entire ordeal brought unbearable pain to all our family.

In life, we know people come and go all the time, but it's only a reality when it happens to someone close to us. When we see others losing their loved ones, we never quite get the full measure until death knocks on our door. Why does there have to be so much hurt? I was breaking down inside. This was my first time experiencing great loss.

Even though there had been other deaths in the family, this was my granddad, my friend—someone I loved very much. He was the one who had always seen through my walls. He knew all my tricks and could see my internal pain. My grandmother was a tower of strength and faith for us all, but watching her lose the love of her life tore me apart.

I loved my grandfather unconditionally. I felt that he— and the bond we shared—was gone forever. I felt so alone at that point, and my connection to God and my belief system was weak or nonexistent. These things set off my emotions. How was I to understand when I lived a life that was so out of balance?

At the time, I was living in my family home, and as a unit things were hard for us. I grew up in a place where the only emotion I could perceive was anger. I couldn't understand this. What was the missing link in connecting me to my father, mother, and siblings? Why did we fight when we loved one another underneath it all? Why did we hurt one another so much when we loved one another so much more?

My world was confusing and, for me, wanting to run away was my escape. My answer to this at that time was taking drugs and drinking, seeing no value in myself. I grew up thinking we were the only family on the street who fought. If there was an argument in the house at night before I went to bed, I thought the world could hear it, so when I went out the next day I was embarrassed. I thought people knew our business.

All these fears—seeing the world through the eyes of fear and being in a place of fear—left me feeling trapped. Somehow I ended up believing that when we die, that's it. We're done.

Whoever came back from heaven and said it was real? Why does life have no meaning, and who can answer my questions about life? Why was I so hard on myself? How could my life not be the perfect thing it was meant to be? Why did I feel like a failure? Why did I have so much fear? Why could I not feel loved?

The list continued until the day God sent my guardian angel to intervene. The only way God could truly intervene would be to answer me when I asked for his help. Don't we all ask these questions at some point in our lives? For some of us, it's more real than others, this feeling that we are all separate from all things in the world, and most of our teachings back this up. From children we are taught that God is separate; God will punish you if you don't love him, or he will send you to hell if you're a sinner. We are all asking the same questions, and trust me, we are all receiving the same answers. It's time to help you to take down the veils of disillusion.

There is a God, but God is so personal to you that only you will ever truly understand. God is unconditional love, there to guide you every step of your way, but you have to always remain true to him. The one true meaning of this is that you, and you alone, hold the truth. So it's time for you to look deep within. The answers you seek you shall find.

I spent the months following my grandfather's death stuck in an emotional rut, the same one I was in for most my young adult life. I was in a not-so-happy relationship. After Christmas 2000, the relationship started to fall apart; it was ending. The feeling of being rejected was really tough, and my inner child was taking a beating with all the different emotions. The real cause for this at the time was that I didn't know how to love myself.

My grandfather's passing gave me the reason I needed to stop taking drugs. This was a major step for me as taking drugs wasn't part of the life I thought I would live. I felt so much better after giving up drugs, but the label would not leave me as easily. I was trying to change my life.

If I went to a bar on a night out there were always people taking drugs, and people would sometimes approach me to ask me to score drugs for them. This was the ultimate discomfort for me. I wanted to leave this behind, but I just couldn't seem to get away from it.

And that became even harder when love left my side. The relationship ended sometime in the early part of 2001. I felt so alone, looking for an escape route and the answers to all my problems. I wanted to run away because I didn't know how to deal with my emotions. I will always remember my grandfather saying to me, "Robert, don't waste your lifetime down here. You have great potential, and it's important for you to know this. No matter where you go in the world, don't be an asshole, because you will always be guaranteed to meet one." On hearing his words playing in my mind, I knew I wanted to change my life but didn't know how. What I did know was that I had to do *something*.

In April 2001 I lost my friend Packie in a motorbike crash, which was another major blow for me as well as for my best friend, Lee, who was the last person to see our buddy alive. I had been with him a couple of days beforehand.

My whole family gathered around me. I was volatile at the time, but I managed to hang in there and battle through the pain. My best friend also needed me because he was blaming himself. I felt angry about losing Packie; he was such a bright young soul and had everything to live for. I found myself facing this internal anger. I can't say it was aimed at God because, up until this point, I had only the Catholic church's teaching of what God *was*—an external power to be afraid of or obey, or to subject to others beliefs or dogma—not what God *is*.

This made me face my own mortality and think on a deeper level about life and death. Either way, I thought I was damned if I did and damned if I didn't.

2

A Phone Call from America

I was at home one evening in early June 2001, and my phone rang. It was my longtime friend Neala, with whom I hadn't spoken for a while. We used to share a house with some friends in our hometown. About a year or so earlier, she had packed her bags and boarded a plane to go and live in New York.

We chatted away on the phone. "What are you doing with your life? Are you still partying?" she asked me.

"No, I'm not. I'm not working full-time at the moment, but I'm done partying. I want to move on with my life," I replied.

"Well, why don't you come and live in New York? It will be a fresh start," she said.

"How will I manage that?" I asked. "What will I do about a job or visa?"

"Oh, don't worry about that. That's a minor detail. We can sort that when you get here. Everyone does. Come over on a holiday visa and see if you like it here. After all, it is the land of opportunity. It's a no-brainer to come and live here with me. It will be like old times," she said.

I laughed as we said goodbye and set down the phone.

I was excited at the thought, but I also felt great fear. However, at this particular time, it was the only option I could see. I decided to take her up on her offer and then started thinking of how I was going to pay for the trip. *How will I get a job?* I thought. *When I get there, what will I do?* I'm a welder by trade so I was sure I would find something when I got there. *It'll be fine,* I thought.

There was no planning and even less thought put into this move. It was my great escape, my golden ticket to the Wonka factory. It was my chance to change my life, get away from my past, start afresh, and live the dream in the Big Apple.

Within a month or so, I was boarding a plane for New York. I didn't have much money to get me there, about seven hundred dollars in my pocket, which was very little in the grand scheme of things. I wasn't really thinking ahead. Going to the States on a holiday visa and finding a job was a spur-of-the-moment decision. But I was escaping. It was exciting. My life was changing and starting to look up!

Before I was to leave for New York, my shoulders, back, and neck seized up. I was in so much pain and told my mom that I didn't think I could go. Mom told me to try some painkillers, which I did, but the pain kept getting worse. It was like all the stress in the world just hit me at once, and my body decided it had had enough. While all this pain was going on, I started to think about my brothers and sister, whom I loved so much—especially my little brother

Jason, the youngest by ten years. We had such a special friendship and bond as brothers.

Some part of me knew that when I left, I would not see Jason as a child anymore. He would be a man when I came home because I was planning to move to the United States, and I knew it would be a very long time before I returned.

The day I was scheduled to leave, my mom asked me, "Are you able to fly? If you're that bad, why don't you give our neighbor a shout. She does massage and healing."

"Healing? What do you mean?" I asked.

"Just go down and ask what she can do to help you," answered my mother.

So I went down and knocked on the door, and my neighbor answered. "Hello! I'm flying to America today, and I've been in so much pain with my back and neck that I can't turn my head. Can you help?" I asked.

"I'm really sorry," she replied, "but I'm booked up for the next few days."

"Okay, thanks for your help," I said. I turned around and started to walk down her drive. Just as I was about to walk out the gate, she called after me.

"Robbie?"

"Yes?"

"Can you come back in an hour?"

"Of course, I can," I replied. "I will see you then. Thank you."

When I got home, my family and friends were coming and going from the house. My best friend Lee was there. We have been friends for the best part of our lives and have been through a lot of things together. Lee was such a great friend. He knew I didn't have much money, so he gave me a helping hand. "Make sure you look after yourself. I will miss you. And whatever you do, stay out of trouble." They were his parting words.

Mom and Dad were very quiet, which was unusual for them. Their way of trying to connect with me was by joking or some other form of humor. This was their way of saying that they loved me. I most definitely didn't have the emotional skills to say I loved them either, nor did I have any true understanding of the meaning of the word *love*. I was still trying to discover the depth of love within myself.

One hour later, I went back to my neighbor's house, feeling very apprehensive. "Make your way upstairs, turn right, and go into the small room," she said. It was what we would call the box room. "I will be with you in a minute."

I went upstairs, and this conversation started again in my mind. *What am I doing? What is this healing going to do? This is a load of crap!* On the other hand, I was in so much pain that I could hardly turn my neck. As I was thinking, she came into the room and said, "Now what's going on with you? How can I help?" I explained what was wrong. I got onto the specialized bed, and she started to use some essential oils. I will never forget the heat from her hands. But for me at this time, that's all it was—heat.

An hour passed. I was half asleep when she said, "I'm finished." I thanked her greatly and left. Walking from her home, I felt instant relief; the heat was unreal. I felt so happy. *America, here I come!* I thought. (The angels were already helping and getting me prepared before I went to America. It's a pity I just wasn't awake to that at this time.

My awakening is written on the stones of life, and those stones would turn to face the son of God, Jesus Christ, when I needed him most.)

At this time, my blinders were truly on, and I had no understanding of how my life was going to change. The son, brother, and friend that my family would all see leaving the country would never be the same again. Saying goodbye was hard but not as hard as I thought. I needed to get away.

On August 3, 2001, I landed at JFK airport. I'd arrived! I will never forget that day. I was nervous going through immigration. *What if they check my bag?* My bag was packed to live in the States, not just visit, so I had packed winter clothes even though it was the middle of summer, with 90% to 100% humidity. I had a lot of my personal stuff with me: music, pictures, and most of what I thought had meaning for me. I was on a holiday visa but had my bags packed for a longer stay!

The first week wasn't too bad. I was having a blast living in the boogie-down Bronx—it was the most amazing place I had ever seen. I hadn't brought the right clothes, which sucked, but it was a great adventure and a whole new life experience. I would travel into Manhattan to see Neala at her place of work, which was a bar just off Times Square. I would take the subway, and that was an experience in itself! I had to start looking for work, and this meant staying in the Bronx. So I would spend most days on my own. I bought phone cards so I could call home—not so much wanting to be home but afraid I was missing something.

Not working made things difficult, and there were some other obstacles to overcome when I first got there. I had nowhere to stay, so I slept on Neala's floor or on the chair in the house she was sharing with some other Irish guys. They didn't mind my staying there for a few nights, but I started to feel the tension. That in itself was hard. I was feeling homesick, and my money was running low. I was so afraid. I couldn't explain the fear I felt. I wasn't going home because I didn't want to be a failure, and I didn't want to go back to Ireland. I really loved the American way and lifestyle, so going home was not an option for me. I was going to make this work no matter what.

At the time, I decided I was going to be happy. I felt like I belonged and nobody knew my past, so it was all good—a fresh start. I was always very independent, and I liked my own company. I would have considered myself prideful at the time, and as the old proverb says, "Pride comes before a fall."

I got up every morning and stood waiting at Sean's Deli, where all the lads would go if they were looking for work. People from various companies would pull up in their vans and ask lads to work. There could be quite a few people waiting there, and I just didn't seem to have success. Most jobs were for bricklayers and carpenters. Welders weren't much in demand, and my confidence was taking a hit. Each morning I felt like crap inside without the support of family or friends back home. This was getting me down, but as usual, I put on a brave face, the mask to hide what was really going on inside.

Neala was there for me when she could be, but she was working a lot of the time so I hid how I was really feeling. Plus, I felt that, because she had family there, she didn't have to worry too much. If anything went wrong, they were there for her. She did support me as best she could, though. What more could she have done for me? But jobs weren't as easy to come by as she had thought they would be. I was losing hope and nearly out of money, so I phoned home.

I spoke to my mom. I made out like I was fine, but I didn't say that I was having trouble finding work.

"Well, you will never guess what," my mom said. "I was talking to Jed, your old boss, and I told him you were in New York. He said his brother is there." Jed had given my mom his brother's name and number so I could ring him for some work. This was the best news ever! I was so happy!

God is always helping us; it's just that we're too
asleep to notice his love and his blessings.

3

Stepping Outside My Comfort Zone

When Neala arrived home, I told her the great news. And she had some good news of her own: she had found us a new place to live. We were moving to East 235th Street. It was a new apartment, and we would be living in the basement. I was super excited! This meant I wouldn't have to sleep on the floor or the couch anymore. Things were starting to look up.

"Are you going to ring that guy?" Neala asked.

"Too right I am," I replied. So I phoned Ray and asked him if he had any work.

"Are you a painter?" he asked.

I said yes, that I had done some painting before but not on a professional level. It was a white lie, but how would he know how foolish I was? Ray lived about fifty miles from me, in a place called Tarrytown. He asked me if I drove in New York, and I told him I didn't. He said he was working on a job close to where I lived and that he would pick me up in the morning. I was over the moon, and so was Neala. Getting work was great news—a lifeline.

I have always had a sense that I am different, but how different still wasn't going to come to light yet. I've had some experiences from when I was a child and into my adult life, but my greater knowing hadn't developed. Everything was still very black and white. The greatest part of me was so different, but I had not opened my heart to God yet and what was within, to express and understand life with such depth and knowing.

Around nine then next morning, Ray called. "Are you ready to work?"

I was thinking, *Yes!* He said, "I'll be there in five minutes."

I was feeling nervous. I thought, *Will I be okay? I hope he doesn't see I'm not a pro. How bad can it be?* I met Ray and found he was a lot like his brother, Jed. He was really down to earth. He asked me if I had ever worked with wood and varnish, but I didn't answer at that point. The house we were going to was very posh, so I thought, *Just take your time and you will be fine.*

When we arrived at the house—which was stunning— Ray explained that he had to go away for a bit. This made me more nervous. We went inside and Ray set me up in the basement, which was finished with lovely wood and had a bar and a pool table. Ray explained that my first job would be to varnish the wood.

"Have you done this before?" he asked me.

"Yes," I answered, very reluctantly.

"Start there. I'll be back in a little while. I have to get supplies."

Oh, God, I was in for it.

I started by lightly sanding the wood. I was used to sanding, so the fun started when it was time to varnish. This had to be done to such a high quality finish, and if I'd known then what I know now, I'd have done things differently. Thinning the varnish down was crucial to make it easier to apply. I didn't know this, so it was like glue—one dip of the brush and the varnish went nowhere. I was frantically trying to spread it but not getting anywhere, so I panicked. I decided to work on the windows, where there was less wood. I thought they would be easier. But after making a mess there too, I thought, *Maybe not.* Well, this was the ending for me.

I was saying to myself, "Please, something go right." But the next minute, I was getting varnish not only on the wood but on the glass as well. I was now fully panicking, sweating, and praying Ray wouldn't come back anytime soon. As soon as those thoughts went through my head, I heard Ray's voice. "Robbie, where are you?" he shouted.

"I'm down here," I answered, my heart racing and my face as red as a beetroot.

Ray walked in, took one look at me, and said, "You're some painter. Are you finished this already?"

I thought, *What do I say? Do I say yes? This is my first day. What if I get sacked?*

Then Ray said, "You've done really well. I'll finish here. There's rubbish and brushes that have to be cleaned up. You go up and look after that and take your time."

Call it whatever you like, but at this point, without my awareness, God was saying to me, *You're okay, Robbie. Things will work out. I have a plan for you.* I wasn't up to the standard of a painter. Ray, on some level, definitely took pity on me, and it was his kindness that got me through the next week or so. Even when he had no real work for me, he always found something to keep me going.

Was luck in my favor? Were my angels looking after me? Or was I just being prepared for my real reason for being in America? I wasn't sure. Remember, I was still not really aware on my journey. As I look back now, I can see the glimmers of light that were shining for me. This is before what I would come to call my true awakening.

So I spent a short time working for Ray, knowing that I would have to look for something more permanent. Work was starting to dry up, so I started looking for other jobs. Neala and I moved into our new apartment. I loved the new place and having my own space. But there was news to come.

Neala arrived home one evening and told me she had a friend coming over. That's all I really knew at the time. I didn't mind too much. I was making new friends, including a few lads living above us.

They were all working and said they would help me find some work. The best way to find a good job, they said, was to play Gaelic football. Growing up I had no love for any kind of football, so this was going to be a challenge.

The lads got me a contact number for one of the football players. I phoned him, and he asked me to come train with the team. I had to go out and buy boots and some other stuff, but to put it plainly, I have two left feet. Having grown up with a father who had managed every football team in my town and successfully helped bring them many cups and trophies, you would think I was a football ace. But it was definitely a case of fake it till you make it.

"Are you working?" one guy asked me one evening.

"No," I answered.

"What kind of work do you do?" he proceeded.

"I'm a welder."

"Are you? One of the lads on the team might know someone looking for a welder. Hold on and I'll find out." He came back with a number and told me to ring them.

Things were looking up. I made the phone call and got offered a job with a massive company as a welder. This was music to my ears. I was still on my holiday visa and now working a full-time job—how crazy is that? I was starting to make some friends locally, which definitely made life seem easier, and getting a new job was another success. The hours were long, but the money was great. It was a win-win!

I was busy with my new job, and life was good. Neala's friend, a girl from the same town as me, would be arriving soon, and Neala told me her friend was bringing a friend. I thought this was great but was unaware that they would be moving in with us. The problem here was that we lived in a two-bedroom apartment. I was working really hard, as was Neala.

I asked Neala, "Where are the girls going to stay?"

"I was thinking your room, and you could take the living room," she replied.

I was fuming and said I couldn't do that. I was getting up at 5:00 a.m. and doing ten- to twelve-hour shifts a day to pay the rent. Living in a living room was not an option. I wasn't going to do it.

I'd shared a room for most of my life, and for me it was important to have my own space. Don't ask me why I was so set on not giving up my room, but it just felt right to me. I paid the bills, and I wanted a bed.

The girls arrived, and it turned out they didn't mind sharing the living room. In fact, we all had a ball living together. Times were good, but the clock was ticking. Little did we know that we were all going to have to face a decision that we never thought we would. This would be a moment in time that would change us all and one that would change the world forever. But before I bring you to this part of my journey, I'm going to rewind the clock a bit.

My Path Before I Knew My Path

In order to go forward in life, sometimes we have to go back. I often tell this story about the path I was on before I woke up. This was an important part of my path, and I can see that now. It showed me that God had always been with me, just like he is with you, but it's amazing how blind we can be.

I was roughly nineteen when I went to see a lady who read from a deck of playing cards. We'd heard from other friends about this lady, and I wanted to see what my future would hold. Was I going to be rich? Be happy? Own my own house? All the usual stuff. In my youthful ignorance, I was unaware at the time that the usual stuff was not the important stuff. As I look back now, I can see that the things we deem important are often simply meaningless possessions. There's way more to life than that.

When we arrived at the lady's home, she opened the door. She reminded me of my grandmother, my mom's mother. She said, "Come in, son." She showed me through to a bedroom, and I took a seat on a chair at the edge of the bed.

She shuffled her cards and started to read. She gave me a great smile and said, "You have had a very traumatic life up to this point, and I see so much pain and hurt around you. I have to tell you that your mother loves you and always will. But your mother has gone through a lot of pain herself. Your immune system has suffered for many years, with chest infections and so on."

This was all true. I had suffered for a good part my life with these symptoms.

"The reason for this is because you carry all the hurt and pain, not only from this lifetime but from others."

Now at this point, I was starting to judge because I had only a little understanding of this life, never mind past ones! The skeptic in me came out, or maybe this was a defense mechanism.

The next thing I remember her saying was, "You will go to America to get away from Ireland, but you will never be the same man coming home, Robert. You have a gift. You're a very powerful healer, but your fear will hold you back."

I was thinking, *What a load of crap. I will never live in America! Gifted—what does that mean?* But at the time, I was so out of touch that there wasn't a hope in the world of me seeing clearly.

My reading was coming to an end. She said, "Don't be afraid of your blessings; these come from God. There will be many who will stand in your way, be jealous, will not be able to understand you or what's truly in your heart. In time, they will see. Remember, if you don't give up, you will be one day living in your deepest truth."

Like anything else in life, when you look back on something, you don't always see the true value of it unless you are fully awake and in the moment. Most people aren't, and it's the inward journey that will bring you to the true value of your life and its meaning.

What is our life without meaning?
Who writes the rules we live under? I ask again.

4

The Day the World Stood Still

September 11, 2001

Most people remember this date, where they were, and exactly what they were doing—or what they *stopped* doing.

I got up on the morning of September 11 and got ready for a normal day at work. For me this day felt a little different, but I can't explain what I felt inside. It was really calm, the sun was shining, and it was predicted to be a hot day. I got dressed for work and made my way down to Sean's Deli to get my coffee and breakfast roll before I got picked up for work. Sean's Deli was really busy, as usual at that time of the morning, with vans and lads coming and going. A lot of lads were making their way to different parts of the city to work.

I chatted with some of the lads I saw there most mornings. A little later, my van pulled up, and off I went to the job, where the bricklayers were already working.

The foreman of the job—who was Irish—asked me to look after some jobs first thing.

"Yes, that's no problem," I replied. "I'm just going to set up."

Now, for some strange reason, I got ready to work as usual, but it took me longer than usual. Not paying any attention to the time, one of the lads came over. "We're sending one of the lads to the shop to get some breakfast stuff. Do you want anything?" he asked.

"Yes, can you get me a drink? A Gatorade or something?" I asked.

I was setting up, but I was also going up and down the stairs to the basement to take some measurements. A truck would be bringing steel later that day, and other supplies were scheduled to be delivered. I was working away when I heard the foreman, "Your drink is here!"

It was roughly eight twenty. We all sat down, and everyone was having a laugh. We were still waiting on the delivery, so I asked the foreman, "What time will the steel be here?" I was waiting on the material. The time was 8:47 a.m.

Everyone's phones started going crazy all of a sudden; there was something going on downtown. The foreman called the driver, who said, "I'm stuck in midtown. They're saying a small plane just hit the North Tower of the Twin Towers."

The foreman said, "We have lads down that far. I will ring and see what they know." Everyone else was still working but talking about this plane.

At this point, we decided we would all chip in and buy a radio so we could hear what was happening at the towers.

When I think back about some of the lads complaining about having to chip in five dollars each to buy a radio, I feel really annoyed. I know this sounds trivial, but as people, we just don't think.

Some messages were getting through, and we learned that it was a bigger plane that had hit the North Tower. Now I was starting to feel that something was not right here, and some of the other lads were thinking the same.

No one knew what to say or do. A small plane sounded bad, but then when word started coming back that it was a bigger plane. And when word reached us that most of the fire stations in the Bronx were now empty, we knew it was a lot worse than we had first thought.

I thought, *What's keeping the lad with the radio?* I looked at my watch. It was 9:04 a.m. A call came through that another plane had just crashed into the South Tower. I said, "Oh, my God." Everyone was panicking, and no one knew what to do. My mind was racing. *Is this a world war? Am I going to see my family again?*

I was filled with panic and fear. The lads were asking the foreman, "What will we do? Will we work on?" I went to my gang box and started to put stuff away, but the foreman asked what I was doing.

I replied, "This is not right. I don't feel safe, and nobody knows what's really happening." He suggested that we wait and see, but I felt this urge to go. I stopped putting away the stuff, and I called it: "I'm getting out of here. I'm going to make my way back to the Bronx. Don't worry about the tools. Who's going to take them?" And with that, everyone downed their tools, and we all left for our homes.

On the drive back, we saw people on the streets crying. It was so surreal. This perfect day had just turned into hell, and it was only the beginning. The smoke in the sky, the pure madness on the streets—it was like a war zone. For many thousands of people, it would be a day of tremendous loss and grief. For a lot more, it was the beginning of the next part of our evolution.

When I arrived back to the Bronx, I started seeing friends and familiar faces on the street. I made my way back to my apartment, wondering if Neala was safe. She worked in the city. I went down my stairs to see if all the girls were home. They were all there, and I was so happy. We were all in total shock. It's so hard for me to describe—it was like being stuck in a Hollywood horror movie and we were just waiting to see the titles come up on the screen. I felt I was stuck in this dreamlike state, feeling so numb and thinking of all those poor people in the towers and the poor souls who were jumping to their deaths and the whole world tuning in on their TV sets. Crazy!

Someone wake me up please. Is this real?

We were safe, but my thoughts were with those people who were trapped in the buildings and the heroes who were giving their lives to save others. There were so many forms of bravery being exhibited.

In the middle of all this madness, we started wondering if any other attacks were taking place. Just then, there was a newsflash: "Breaking News."

Another plane had crashed, but this time into the Pentagon. I was really worried because the media were only showing what was happening in America. I felt we had no connection to the rest of the world. *What else is happening around the world? Will I see my family again? Is this World War 3?* That was all I could think of, and for that moment I had to try and set aside all feelings that were not of love and any battles from the past that had no meaning. It was just important to connect to my loved ones again, to let them know I was safe but also to make sure they were safe as well.

The phone in our apartment wouldn't call out, so I decided to make my way back out on the streets to find a pay phone to ring home.

When I got down to Katona Avenue, I found queues to use the pay phones. Because of the influx of calls from cell phones, the networks had gone down. I joined the queue to phone home.

At 9:58 a.m., the first World Trade Center tower crumbled to the ground. There was a great feeling of urgency to call home, to tell my parents I was safe. I stood in the queue in total shock, looking at people's crying faces—we were all over the place. I just couldn't believe this. Who would attack America? This superpower? The land of the free? I had always believed that this country was untouchable; the reality was that it wasn't.

The experience brought home the fact that we're all so vulnerable, and there is always a reason for the moment. You are always where you are meant to be, and there is no way to escape what your journey has chosen for you. It was at this moment I prayed to God: *Please let me be safe.*

What I have to explain, though, is my understanding in life at that time. I believed that people should pray to God only when they were in trouble or had done something wrong. Otherwise, we shouldn't waste God's time. One of the reasons I felt totally separate from God was that I had little or no belief at that time. Somewhere deep, deep within, I had faith, but that faith wasn't to be found on the outside!

At 10:15, my turn came to make a call. I tried to phone home but couldn't get through. It was just after three o'clock in the afternoon in Ireland, and all phone lines seemed to be jammed. This day felt unreal, and as I looked around the street, I wasn't sure if this was the end. Not getting through on the phone annoyed me, but there was little I could do. I decided to try again later.

As I stood on the street talking to people, I heard all kinds of stories from people who had friends and family in the towers. What do you say? Tell them you hope they'll be okay? Words meant nothing to those terrified people, and they probably never will.

I made my way back to our apartment in about ten minutes, and this really bad feeling came over me. We were all looking at the TV and—*crash!* There went the second tower. I felt numb and was fighting back tears. I knew that my life and our world were changing on this day. It would never be same again, and for me, it would be the starting event to point me toward my awakening. But I didn't know yet that my awakening was coming.

I finally got in contact with my family. My relief at hearing their voices was fantastic. "I was so worried. We all were," Mom said to me. She asked me what I was going to do, suggesting that it would be safer if I came home. I didn't know what I was going to do. I felt torn. I thought, *What's going to happen?* I wasn't sure, but I had this deep feeling and desire to stay. My journey in the States wasn't over yet.

I told my mom that I would give it a few days before deciding what to do, but first I had to chat to Neala and see what she was going to do. In the immediate aftermath, every TV station just replayed the terrible footage from that day. It was becoming like the movie *Groundhog Day,* and I was getting numb to it all. I decided that I wasn't going to watch TV anymore. I felt the pain of all the people hurting in my heart. Plus, the media were war-mongering, which made everything scarier.

People were so angry, hurt, and in pain—I could see and feel it. *Why am I going through this?* I thought. *Why am I feeling so sensitive to people's pain again? I can't understand.* My mind felt clouded, and I was extremely sensitive to a lot of things. The feelings I experienced were a lot like those I'd had in my childhood. I didn't have the tools to express how I felt, so I did what I had always done—suppressed my feelings. I hid away and continued with life, plowing my way through it. I buried my head and just moved forward.

Things were really hard, not just for me but also for the girls I lived with and the people of New York. I wasn't too sure if I would stay or go back home. The feeling of being a failure wasn't long in creeping in, and going home became a moot option for me. My pride or ego was doing all the talking, and I felt that I had no choice but to stay. If I went back to Ireland, I felt, I would have no life or meaning.

I asked Neala, "What are we going to do?" She was also unsure what to do, but I knew in my heart she didn't want to go home.

In the following days I returned to work, taking my mind away from what was going on in the world. I started using drink as a way of escape, a crutch, my way of hiding many feelings and emotions. It was a case of sticky plaster syndrome: you stick a plaster on the problem to cover the cuts and bruises, but eventually, the plaster will fall off and the wounds will be revealed.

We were all trying to get our lives back to normal, but with four of us in a two-bedroom apartment, things felt very claustrophobic. Since I had grown up sharing a room with two brothers, I was used to having people around, but it was starting to get a little hard for me. With my male energy combined with three female energies, different opinions and feelings were bound to surface.

I tried my best to work through them, but inside I felt like I was a kettle coming to the boil. But I kept a brave face to avoid any arguments.

The conversation with Neala came up again: were we going to stay or go? We both decided then and there that we would stay. For me, when I made this decision, that was it. I was going to make a life here and find all the happiness I had been looking for. It's a tough place to live, but if you're a fighter you can survive.

It was Friday—payday. I was feeling good and was going places. Evening was approaching, which was also pay time! The way we got paid was like something you would see in *The Godfather*. The boss would come in with a huge bag of cash, sit in the corner with the foreman, call our names, and when we went over, he opened the bag and handed us envelopes stuffed with cash. This was such an amazing feeling. I was on top of the world, and it felt like my life had a flow to it.

When my name was called, I went over to the boss. As he paid me, he asked if I would be interested in working on the upcoming Saturday and Sunday for him. (But it wasn't really a question!) He emphasized how important this job was and told me I would be paid well. So of course I said yes—my boss engendered a bit of fear. I was also a people pleaser and didn't want to let him down. I will never forget him saying to me, "Don't let me down. I'm really relying on you, Robbie, so don't go on the beer. I have a lot of men coming tomorrow, and it's important that you're here." This man didn't give people a verbal sacking if they let him down. It was more of a physical one, and I knew this to be true. There was no way in the world I was going to let him down—or so I thought!

I had been paid, it was close to the end of our workday, and those who were working Saturday and Sunday could go home. We packed up our gear, and I jumped into the van with the lads and headed back to the Bronx. The vans would drop us off at a place on MacLean Avenue, where there were quite a lot of pubs. I had every intention of going home, but some of the lads who were going for drinks asked me to join them. I had initially said no as I was working the next day, but they were very insistent that I come along.

They were a friendly bunch of lads, so I agreed to go for a bottle; I also wanted to be part of the peer group. It was around five o'clock, and I thought, *Surely one or two bottles won't do any harm.*

I thought I would be home by about six-thirty, which turned into nine, and before I knew it, it was after eleven. At this point you can imagine the state I was in. But the lads kept buying rounds, and I kept knocking them back—as one does when one has a 5:00 a.m. start the next day!

It was roughly three in the morning when I returned to my apartment. Neala was very annoyed with me for being in such a state. She was only looking out for me, worrying about my work. I reassured her that I would be fine and went to bed, but about twenty minutes later I started to feel very ill. Without warning, I became violently sick. Now, I'm not the biggest drinker in the world, so it could have been alcohol poisoning, but I still have no real clue what all that was about.

I slept through the alarm because I was so incapacitated from the drink and lack of sleep. Because I felt so sick, I wallowed in my own self-pity but also felt depressed about drinking and guilt-ridden for not turning up for work.

What have I done?

I had landed this great job, made a promise to the boss, and then let him down. I spent all that day in bed and slept into Sunday. But instead of biting the bullet and getting up for work on Sunday, I couldn't do it. I was so fearful about the silly mistake I had made. I was beating myself up so much that the Sunday led to Monday and then Tuesday.

At this point, I was in a place that I didn't know how to get out of. Neala started to ask questions about my absence from work. The pressure from this lay heavily on my shoulders, and I didn't know how to tell her that the reason I hadn't gone into work was that night of beer drinking, even though she probably knew. She tried to persuade me to ring my boss and ask if I could return to work, but I couldn't do it. I was just too afraid.

Looking back, I know that the fear I felt back then stemmed from my childhood fears. There was a part of me that lost this communication ability. I didn't know how to communicate. It's hard to explain what was going on inside, but I knew that I had to get myself out of the situation. I hadn't left the house for four days, so on Wednesday morning, I plucked up the courage to go down to Sean's Deli.

I kept thinking, *Please don't let me meet any of the lads or bosses from work.* Walking down toward the deli, I hung my head between my shoulders in case I met anyone I knew. There was a part of me saying, *If I meet anyone, let the ground open up and swallow me please.*

As I was standing in the deli queue talking to a couple of the lads, I heard the door open and looked behind me. It was the foreman. The blood just drained out of me, and I could feel my knees knocking. My heart was pounding. As I plucked up the courage—with a whimper in my voice—to say hello to him, he gave me a dirty look and completely ignored me.

At this point I wished I were six feet under. I paid for my food and started to make my way back to the apartment when, out of nowhere, I had this conversation in my head. *Go back down and talk with him. At least apologize.* So I turned on my heels and went back, not knowing what I was going to say.

As I came around the corner, the foreman was coming out of the deli. I approached him and, just as I was about to speak, he started shouting at me. "You let us all down, Robbie! Why didn't you turn up for work? You knew you weren't going to come in, so why didn't you just ring? We all felt so let down by you. Plus we had to ring someone else to come in and do your job."

I just stood there feeling awful inside. I really felt like crying, especially after beating myself up inside for the last four days and knowing I had let myself down. "I'm sorry," I said.

"Sorry just doesn't cut the mustard around here," he replied. He could see my eyes welling up, and I also felt that he knew I wasn't a bad person, that I was a hard worker who had just made a mistake. "Those lads that you had drinks with turned up for work. They are seasoned drinkers, and you're a good lad, but don't get caught up in that way of life here. I've seen so many lads come over from Ireland and do the same," he told me. He was giving me some good advice, and inside I knew that this was my truth. "We all make mistakes. I will make a phone call, but I can't promise you anything. Be at the deli tomorrow morning. Be ready for work—but I can't say if I will have work for you."

"Thank you," I said, and again I apologized for letting them down.

"I will see you in the morning."

I went home and never slept a wink that night because of worry. I tossed and turned; my mind was racing, and my heart was pounding. Why do we do this to ourselves or choose this experience in our lives? It's horrible, but this seems to be something we put ourselves through.

The next morning arrived, and I made my way to the deli. The van pulled up, and the boys asked me to jump in. I was delighted. At the job site, I waited for the boss to come in, but I had my guard up. It had never been my intention to miss work or let the company down. This was just a cycle that was going on in my life, and I didn't have the tools to break it. I have worked in so many jobs throughout my life, but I could never seem to find the perfect balance.

I have always felt like I had more to offer and that there was more to me, but I didn't know how to explore this fully. A lot of this inability came from my childhood and young adulthood.

Anyway, I was down in the basement welding some steel and working away, when suddenly, I stopped, lifted my welding shield, and there he was—the boss, who was known for having a bit of a temper. Well, the blood just drained out of me. He was walking toward me, and the look on his face wasn't a happy one. At this point, I thought, *Oh, please God, get me out of this. I promise I won't mess up again. Please! I swear!*

He gave me a warning stare and then just walked right past me. I felt relief right away. Just as I was thinking this, he walked back over to me. *This is it. I'm in trouble now.*

"Oh, you decided to turn up did you?" he asked.

I simply replied, "Yes," with a look of terror on my face.

I was just about to grovel when he added, "You let me down and the lads that turned up for work. Drink can be the ruination of any man. You're a good chap and a hard worker. This will be your first and last chance with me, so keep your head down and go back to work. Oh, and by the way, it took a lot courage to come back to work." And with that he was gone. Relief!

I felt like all my Christmases had come at once. I felt so much better at that moment; my life was back on track, and I still had a job. Even though I was only on a holiday visa and shouldn't have been working, it was the only way I could see forward.

As the weeks passed, I began to think more of home. I was really missing my family and friends and feeling lonely. But I just kept my head down and tried to look ahead in a positive way.

America was growing on me day by day, and for the first time in my life I had this feeling of being in the right place at the right time. The city had so much to offer. I was working really long hours, but I was making a few dollars. This was just the way of life in America, and you either loved it or hated it. It had this magnetic hold on me, and without realizing it at the time, the intuitive reading I had gotten all those years ago with the old lady had proven true. I was living the dream—the American Dream, like so many before me had done and so many after me will do.

There was, however, still an air of hostility in America and a lot of talk about war and terrorists. We were still on high alert and under threat of attack. Lower Manhattan, which had now become ground zero, had its own battles, namely looking for survivors, or at least the remains for the families so they could get closure. This would prove to be a painstakingly slow process as there was so much rubble and debris to work through.

I remember traveling downtown to Lower Manhattan. When I got close to where the World Trade Centers had stood, the smell of burned rubble penetrated my senses. This feeling was eerie. Plus seeing the tributes and all the pictures of the people who had lost their lives really affected me. Even writing about this now, I feel a great wave of emotion for that time.

There was a threat of chemical warfare, and *anthrax* soon became the word that was on everybody's mind. There was just so much uncertainty. I could feel this change in my life, and for many others, a wave of change was happening in the world.

America is a special place to me—such a magical land— but the threat of anthrax was very real and scary, and the media totally played up the fear. The world we were living in was undergoing change, and it was the beginning of this war on terror. *If America is not safe, where is?* I thought. This was the driving force for my fear.

For me, it was just a matter of keeping my head down and moving forward. After all, I'm Irish, and this was something many generations had done.

It was kind of weird, though. I was in the States on a holiday visa, working and thinking of staying. The weeks were passing, and I was coming close to the expiration date of my visa. After 9/11, security was stepped up, and immigration officers conducted a number of raids on building sites, homes, and bars. We were all hearing horror stories about people getting caught and sent home with a five- or ten-year ban on returning.

I spoke to Neala. We had so much to think about. She traveled to the bar where she worked off of Times Square every day, and police and immigration officers were now stopping people on trains and buses. It was a funny place to find yourself. I hadn't gone to the States with the intention of breaking the law, but I was just about to. To go home at this point wasn't an option. It was fight or flight. What would *my* choice be?

5

Treading the Thin Line

November 4, 2001

My three-month visa was on its last legs, and I knew that talking to Neala would make my choice a lot easier. From the next day on, I would be classed as an illegal alien and would have to be so much more careful. What must I have been thinking? This meant no bank accounts, no driver's license, and no real medical care.

Everything had to be paid for in cash. The reality was that there was no going home. The choice was made. The die was cast!

Christmas was fast approaching, and we were all getting in the holiday mood. Neala was going to cook Christmas dinner, and I was really looking forward to some good home cooking. It was snowing, and the weather was pretty harsh. It was my first time to experience snow for more than a couple weeks, and at the beginning it was fun having to dig ourselves out of the snow. But it wasn't long before it lost its magic. Don't get me wrong—I like the snow, but I am not a lover of it. Being born in the middle of summer, I always loved those golden rays of sunshine.

But at this point, Christmas fever had well and truly set in. It was such an amazing sight to see all the Christmas lights and how people decorated their homes. Fifth Avenue was just amazing, including the world-famous ice rink at Rockefeller Center, which has become a quintessential symbol of New York City winter. It has a fairy-tale feeling to it that brings out the inner child in people.

Christmas Day arrived, and I was looking forward to dinner with Neala and her boyfriend, Rob, and calling my family to wish them a happy Christmas. It is a big day for our family in Ireland. Everyone would go to our grandmother's. The adults would play cards, and all the grandchildren would play with whatever Santa had brought them. It was always a great occasion. I don't know how my grandmother coped with so many grandkids running around, but then again, my granny had the patience of a saint! What an amazing lady, with a faith so strong. She prayed for everyone in the family. We always say her prayers would be heard throughout heaven. She was a very wise lady.

Back in New York, Neala was cooking, I opened a beer, and we exchanged presents. I phoned home and chatted with my mom. I asked, "How are Jason, Joey, and Vicky?"

"They're good," she replied.

"How's Dad? Has he gone to work?" My dad drove a taxi and would always work on Christmas Day after dinner.

Neala shouted, "Ask your mom how to speed up the roast potatoes!"

As I was having this conversation, I realized how much I missed my mom's Christmas dinner. My mom is an amazing cook. She told me to tell Neala to baste a small drizzle of oil over the roast potatoes and to turn the oven temperature a little higher. We had been getting this funny smell in the apartment since a few days earlier, but we really didn't think too much about it. How silly of us!

I was chatting away with Mom when I heard a huge bang followed by a scream. Just then, Neala went running past my bedroom door at ninety miles an hour, screaming her head off.

I said to Mom, "I have to go."

I went to the kitchen and found that our stove was on fire. Rob was beating it with a tea towel, trying to put out the flames. Neala had done as Mom suggested and turned the oven up, and then she had asked Rob to check on the meat and potatoes. What we didn't know at the time was that there was a gas leak at the back of the oven and fumes had built up inside. As Rob opened the oven door, the build-up went *boom!* And he went flying.

Neala panicked and ran upstairs to get help. I can still hear her screaming in my mind. It wasn't funny at the time, but it is funny to look back on. We got the fire sorted, but let's just say that Christmas dinner was off the menu. My first Christmas in New York, and it went off with a bang!

New Year's Eve arrived and Neala was going away, which meant I was home alone. I decided to have a few beers and celebrate by myself. This was my first New

Year's Eve away from home and my first in New York. I should have been out partying, but I was alone and feeling so lonely. I started thinking about my life and where it was going, really trying to find my sense of purpose. I felt isolated with only my dark thoughts.

So there I was in my apartment while most of the people I knew had plans. For me, this was the start of feeling like I didn't want to live. *What is wrong with me?* I asked myself. Feeling lonely and isolated, these emotions hit me all at once. I had come here to find happiness but felt like crap inside, and all I wanted to do was to take my own life.

I was so lost inside. I was angry; my life had no meaning—that's what my brain was telling me. There was a battle going on in my mind, with one half saying, "Do it—take your life," and the other giving me every reason not to. I tried to suppress those feelings. I needed to put them back into the dark hole they had come from and continue with life as if it were perfect: always smiling on the outside but inside in complete turmoil.

Why has this wave of great sadness come over me? What is wrong with me? As I asked myself this question, I started to cry, thinking, *I hate myself.* The feeling of guilt was overwhelming.

I went to the bathroom, and as I looked into the mirror, I asked myself, "Who am I? What am I? Why do I hate myself? Why is this place I find myself in so painful?"

6

The Mirror

I was looking into the mirror at this person looking back at me. I didn't recognize him! I was crying, and I started to feel this energy around me; it was similar to an energy I used to feel as a child. As I felt it with me again, I didn't fully understand it, but the feeling of wanting to kill myself wasn't as strong. I knew someone or something was comforting me at that time. I started to feel at ease, and the dark thoughts slipped away. I was still crying, looking at myself, and trying to understand why I had these thoughts and felt this way. I asked myself again, "What's wrong with me?" As I looked into my reddened eyes, I felt this polar shift and my whole body felt lighter. In the next moment, I was taken back to an earlier time. Yes! I was taken out of my body back to a time when I was taking drugs in my local nightclub. I saw myself there, at a rave.

As I looked around, I started to see all the people I had partied with back in the day, filling the nightclub. Everybody was partying. I was with my friends in a part of my life when I had been lost, searching to find who I was in that time. I couldn't see that, though, as the drugs had a great way of hiding all the demons and making it harder to find the part of me I was so longing for.

I saw myself walking to the dance floor, where everybody was bouncing around. I knew most of the people on the dance floor. I started to dance and felt amazing! My body felt so alive. Some guy on the dance floor asked me if I wanted a rush, a term people use to refer to a technique to get themselves higher. There are different types of rushes.

The best way I can explain this is that a person cuts off your blood supply, and you hold your breath for about thirty seconds. They pick you up and then slam you to the floor, giving you a rush of blood to the head. It gets you so high that your brain feels like it is going to explode.

The guy asked me again if I wanted one. I said, "No, I'm feeling really high."

"Are you sure?" he asked. I never answered him. A few minutes later he came back, nagging me, "Come on, have one. You will love it."

I gave in and said, "Don't give me a big rush. I'm feeling a little out of it, and don't let me go!" This guy was really strong and started the process. I said again, "Don't let me go." Next thing I knew, he had picked me up and slammed me down. I wasn't ready or in a good place, but he let me go anyway. I blacked out, and when my feet hit the floor he let go.

I fell straight down and smashed my face into the dance floor. I was gone, knocked out. I left my body for a few brief moments and could see everyone standing around me.

I was looking at myself as I lay on the dance floor. I also saw a massive bright light, and this was no disco light. People were starting to gather around me, and as I came to, the first face I saw was that of a girl from my school days. The look on her face was one of sheer terror.

"Are you okay?" she asked. It looked like she was saying it in slow motion, and as she pointed to my face, I could see a lot of blood but had no idea it was mine.

As I tried to leave the dance floor, people started running over to me, saying, "Are you okay? Look at your face!" I couldn't understand what they were saying, but then someone said, "Get Lee." I heard someone say, "He needs to go to hospital."

I went to the men's room to clean myself up. I stood in front of the mirror looking at my bloody face and thinking, *What have I done to myself now?* I was completely sober and lucid at this point. So many thoughts ran through my mind, worrying about how I was to explain this to my parents— and on top of that, the shame I felt was overwhelming. I took a seat outside the men's room, and someone brought me water and a tissue. I was not in any pain, but I was feeling very shocked. *Why did I allow this insanity to happen to me?* In this instant I could see everything so clearly, and with that came a very real and sane moment.

I started looking around the nightclub and began to see bright-colored lights hovering around people. The lights seemed to be hugging them, keeping them safe. But it took this massive shock for me to see again what I had been seeing as a child, just for that brief moment. When they weren't hovering, they were moving fairly quickly among other people. I could see all these different colors around people, some with shapes and others without.

The colors I was seeing were unimaginable! They were so beautiful, and when they came closer to me, they moved slower and weren't as transparent as when they were moving away—when they moved really fast, the next thing I heard was lots of loud bangs. It was the fireworks outside.

I was back in my body in my apartment and this out of body experience was over. I was looking at the man in the mirror. God was now beginning to reenter my life. I couldn't help thinking about what I had experienced on New Year's Eve, but the fear crept in again just like it had when I was a child.

I suppressed what had happened because I didn't know how to deal with the reality. I locked it away deep within my mind in a place that wouldn't be easy to reach. I was afraid to face my real truth, which was that I had always been connected to God and the angels. These feelings made me look deep inside and question my existence.

January was very quiet workwise, and I was starting to worry about money again. Neala and I were moving to a bigger apartment on the same street, just a few doors away, and the rent was a lot higher, so I felt the pressure. The new apartment was lovely. The only downfall was that the landlord and his family lived beneath us, and that would have its own complications.

Before we moved in, they wanted our passports to photocopy them, for legal reasons. I remember saying to

Neala, "I'm not giving it to them. We will be handed over to immigration if anything goes wrong."

"Don't be silly, Robbie," Neala said. "They won't know you're not meant to be here."

I remember thinking that all they would have to do was read our visa waiver on the passport and we would be goners. But I did trust Neala, and she was very good at making me feel at ease.

I started a new welding job. It was hard work with long hours—all things I was used to. Things were looking up again! But the age-old question was still in the back of my mind: *Will I ever find a job where I fit and can be happy in?*

I started dating a girl named Kim in February 2002. She was like a breath of fresh air to me and great fun to be with. She was of American and Irish descent and came from a good family. She was a well-educated and ambitious woman who worked for a financial company. The first few weeks with Kim were quite challenging. I had to tell a white lie about my residency, saying I had a visa. I was afraid that my being illegal would affect our relationship. I wanted her to get to know me before I said what my true status was. I was working at the time, so she didn't have any reason to question me. I have to say that this was such an amazing time for me and everything was perfect; we were living the dream together.

I would travel into the city most nights to see Kim. She lived in midtown in a beautiful high-rise apartment. It was such an exciting time in my life. She was a kind and caring person, traits that always shone through her.

At one point, I had some issues getting my wages. Kim thought it was strange that I got paid in cash and started asking me lots of questions. She was onto me! I knew I would have to tell her the truth at some stage, but I kept putting it off, afraid that she would run a mile. When we eventually had the conversation, she laughed. "I knew all along, Robbie!"

When I worked in the city, I would travel home on the subway and then get a bus back up to the Bronx. Some days I would stop for a few drinks in a pub called the Catalfo. As we would we say back in Ireland, it was a real spit-on-the-floor pub with the odd fight or two. I played pool and enjoyed the *craic* (an Irish term referring to the entertainment, fun, conversation, and general atmosphere of an event).

While there, I befriended a lovely chap named John. It's funny how the God sends you people or things as you need them without your even knowing the reason. Over the next couple of weeks, I popped in for a few drinks after work. The Irish pubs in the Bronx offered free dinners to get the lads in the door, and it was definitely better than making dinner myself after working a twelve-hour shift!

I met John most days. We would buy rounds of drinks for each other, play games of pool, and put the world to right with our conversations. He was born in Ireland himself, but his family had immigrated to America when he was a child, so we had much in common. We would talk about the "old country," as he liked to call it. We were getting on great; he felt like a big brother to me.

The more I got to know and trust John, the more comfortable I felt sharing my story with him. I remember Kim warning me at the time to be careful, as you never know with whom you're speaking. Never was a truer word spoken!

Without listening to Kim's advice, and with the help of a few pints, my tongue was loose and my guard was down. Before I knew it, I was telling John some hard truths, that I was illegal and working. I wasn't proud of it. John was listening and not saying much.

As John headed to the restroom, the bartender came over to me and said, "I couldn't help but hear what you were saying to John about you being illegal. Do you realize he's a cop, a detective for the NYPD?"

I nearly joined John in the restroom at the shock of hearing this. I felt like I was going to vomit. I had never thought to ask him what he did for a living; I just assumed he was a builder or something. I never questioned why none of the lads sat with him. He was so quiet.

"There is no way he could ever be a cop," I said to the bartender.

"I'm telling you—he is. Be careful. I'm only looking out for you," he replied. "What other person would be allowed to carry a gun into a pub? Look at his hip when he comes out from the restroom."

I couldn't believe it. I was in shock. Before I knew it, the restroom door opened. John came back to his seat beside me, and as he sat down, I got a glimpse of his gun. I was trying to put on a brave face, but I was thinking of doing a Forrest Gump move and running like I'd never run before.

John was chatting as normal. I, on the other hand, was having a complete meltdown, waiting for my chance to bolt out the door. My mind was racing with thoughts of being arrested at my home—I had stupidly told John my address! So, when John walked over to the jukebox, I saw my opportunity and left.

When I arrived back at my apartment, breathless, I told the girls what had just happened. They didn't seem to be too bothered, but I was freaking out, so I decided to stay with Kim for a few nights.

I packed up a bag and headed into the city to Kim's. This would be a welcome distraction—even though we were both worried about my getting found out and the possibility of getting deported. When I stayed with Kim, I felt so good inside, happy that we got on so well together.

After staying at Kim's for a week, I had to go back home to get some stuff for work. As I walked past the deli to my apartment, fate intervened and I bumped into John! I had nowhere to run and nowhere to hide. I had no choice—I had to speak to him.

"What happened to you the other day?" he asked. "I went to put music on, and when I turned around you were gone. I thought I had done something to you. Is everything okay?"

"Yes, I'm fine," I nervously replied.

John went on to tell me that the people behind the bar had told him that they had warned me he was a cop. I confessed that I panicked and thought he was going to hand me in.

John laughed and said that he understood my situation, that he was my friend, and not to worry. But he echoed Kim's advice about being careful with what I said to people. This was a big lesson for me because I'm such an open and trusting person, and I presumed that everyone else would be the same.

"Now let's go for a bottle, buddy," John said. I was so relieved to hear those words.

He later opened up and confided in me that the reason he had never told me he was a cop was because he was struggling with the loss of his brothers after 9/11. The trauma of that day had left great scars on his heart and mind. John was such a strong man, but the pain he was going through was immeasurable.

He phoned me one day and asked if I could come and see him at his apartment—he had something for me. I spent the day wondering what it could be. I was extremely curious and couldn't wait to find out what it was, so I went straight after work that same day.

When I arrived at John's apartment, he was thrilled to see me, giving me a guided tour of his apartment. He loved to play the drums and had an electronic set, which I had never seen before.

John said to me, "I want to give you this card. It's called an NYC PBA Card (for the Patrolmen's Benevolent Association). We only get a few each year to give to our family members. You can use it; if you ever get into trouble, it will help you. If anyone asks where you got it, just say my name, where I work, what department, and you will be okay. Oh, and say you're my cousin."

I was speechless at this point. I had heard about these special cards before. One of the guys I worked with had one. He said it was difficult to get one as only close family members were allowed them. This guy told me he had gotten stopped for speeding once, but when he produced this card, his speeding offense was automatically quashed. He said it was like his get-out-of-jail card.

When John handed me the card, I realized it was a special edition PBA September 11th card, which gave it even more meaning and value. I was so grateful. I thanked him for this thoughtfulness and for looking out for me.

Things always happen for a reason. You always meet the right people at the right time. Divine timing!

Hard Decisions and Life-Changing Choices

The crew and I started a new job in midtown in an army barracks that doubled as a museum. We had to be on site for a set time as we had to get security clearance. If anyone was late and missed the cut-off, that person wouldn't be permitted on the site. Missing a day's wages wasn't an option! It was some setup because we were nearly all illegal, yet we were working in a government building!

Once we got clearance, we went onto the roof and worked there until the shift ended. It was the dirtiest job ever. We had to replace all the fire escapes throughout the building. The weather was turning nice as we were heading for summer, but it was pretty hot up on that roof.

Two laborers, brothers from Guatemala, helped me on the job. The connection they had reminded me of my own two brothers back home in Ireland, whom I missed greatly. The Guatemalans were such hard workers. I mostly welded while the boys ground out the old steel so that the new steel could take its place.

Most of the Latino lads who worked with us weren't treated very well. I helped them a lot more than the other lads did. I really felt for the two Guatemalan brothers. They presented themselves as happy, but the odd time when I looked into their eyes, I could see a great sadness. Like me, these two brothers were living and working in America illegally.

One day, I decided to ask them why they chose America to live and work in. They told me that, back home, they were so poor that they could barely feed themselves, and there was little to no available employment. They felt like they had no choice but to come to America because their lives were so hard. They had my full attention while telling their story. They told me that they had another brother and that the three of them had walked for weeks, sharing one pair of trainers, to get to the border.

"Where is your other brother working?" I asked.

What they told me next was the saddest story I had ever heard. Their brother had died as they were walking to America. They had to make the hardest decision that anyone would ever have to make: whether to leave their brother behind. If they turned and started to walk home with their brother's body, they may not have made it home alive themselves. So they made the difficult decision to continue on their journey to America, leaving their brother's body behind.

I was in complete shock at hearing this horrific story; my heart felt so sad. I couldn't imagine having to do this with my own brothers. I felt grateful and lucky that day for my own family and how much I love them.

This tragic story really made me look at myself and question my purpose in this world. I asked myself, *What am I doing? What is my purpose?* Somewhere deep inside I was looking for answers, but I was not awake enough to receive the understanding or answers I needed at the time.

My introspection was quickly interrupted with the sound of the grinder as the brothers ground and prepared the metal for me. They would never wear masks, which I thought was crazy. I gave them a hand in grinding the metal to speed things up. I had run out of dust masks, so I was completely exposed to the fumes and dust from the abrasive wheel and metal.

What I didn't realize at the time was that the original paint on the old fire escapes was a lead-based paint, which is not good for your health—especially when it heats up because of a grinder and you're breathing in the dark blue smoke that escapes from it. This smoke could cause lead poisoning in the blood. I could feel and taste the smoke and fumes. Thank goodness I was doing this for only a day; the brothers were doing it for a week or so.

When we finished that day, I asked the brothers why they had no masks to wear. They said they were afraid to ask the boss for masks because he might fire them. I couldn't believe it. I thought this was complete madness. I knew right there and then that I would have to do something about this.

I headed over to Kim's apartment after work. On the subway, I felt ill, with the most awful taste in my mouth. When I arrived at Kim's, I sank into the sofa still feeling unwell. Kim rang her father for advice, and he thought it sounded like a touch of lead poisoning. All I could think about was the two brothers. I had to do something about this.

I phoned my boss straightaway. We exchanged a few words, but when I explained everything to him, he said he would have all the proper gear sorted for the next day. Results! I was delighted.

7

Everything Has Its Time and Place

I woke up early the next morning. My stomach had felt sick all night, so I decided I had better call the boss to say I couldn't make it. He was pissed off and threatened me with the sack if I didn't show up for work. Talk about dog-eat-dog. I didn't want to lose my job, but when I told Kim—let's just say she disapproved. I got ready for work in a rush so I wouldn't be late.

Take your time; you will arrive when you arrive!

I was in a panic to get to work on time for the security check. I ran to the subway station on Lexington. Just as I was about to go down the stairs, I felt a very strong presence around me. It felt like a warning. I didn't stop to think or question this feeling.

As I reached the platform, I noticed that all the ticket stalls were packed with huge queues. I looked at my watch to see the time, when I heard a voice in my mind: *Robbie, slow down. Take your time. You will arrive when you arrive.* I never even blinked. Instead I questioned why on earth I was telling myself to slow down, reasoning with my mind. I still wasn't awake or fully aware of my intuition.

I made my way to the queue for my train, and before I knew it I heard it coming. I needed to catch this train in order to get to work on time. I heard the bell that indicated the doors opening: *ding dong.* Then I had a moment of complete madness. I saw an opportunity to get through the gate used for wheelchairs and buggies. I dashed over to the gate, bolted through it, and boarded the train. *Oh, my God, what am I doing?* My heart was pounding out of my chest.

The train was packed, so I had to stand. I had a bag with me with a change of clothes in it. I heard the sound of the door closing: *ding dong.* As the train started to pull off, I had a real sense of relief knowing I had gotten onto the train and would arrive to work on time.

Famous Last Words

While I was standing in the center of the train carriage, I felt the same strong presence that I had felt at the top of the stairs in the train station. It was like I was being warned about something. Before I had time to think about it, a hand rested on my shoulder. I turned around and saw a man holding onto my shirt. I was just about to say, "What do you think you're at?" and push his hand away when I saw him reach around his neck and pull out his police badge.

Oh, no, I thought.

"I'm a transit officer," he began. "I followed you onto to the train at Lexington Avenue. I'm arresting you for not paying to get onto this train. The City of New York doesn't take kindly to these offenses." He handcuffed me and explained that he was taking me downtown to the central police station. I was beyond nervous. Everyone on the train looked at me like I was a terrorist. Talk about shame and embarrassment.

We got off the train at Hunter College. As the doors opened, the officer got on his radio and said, "Central, send a car to pick up at Hunter College."

At this point all I could think of was getting into trouble for being illegal and being sent home. My mind was reeling. *What about Kim and all my belongings in my apartment?* When things like this happen, the officers never take you home to get your stuff. They lock you up, book you on the next available flight, and deport you out of the country.

My thoughts were running wild. *What if they go to my apartment and catch the girls?* I made a decision right there and then that I would not give my real address. The cop was really annoyed and angry with me, saying he was sick of people like me wasting his time when he could be doing more important jobs.

As I listened to him going off, I was beating myself up inside. *How stupid am I? I'm getting what I deserve for not being honest.* My parents had always taught me to be honest—I was brought up with good morals.

We left the train platform, and the cop pointed me toward the street, holding me by the handcuffs behind my back. We got up onto the street, and he started asking questions: "Why did you do that? Have you got ID on you? What's in the bag? Why were you in such a rush?" I didn't know what to say. I was speechless.

A police car pulled up to take me to the station. I started shaking at this point. "What's your name? Have you got ID?" the officer asked.

"I have ID in my back pocket, in my wallet," I replied. The ID I was carrying came from my local police station in Ireland. It is an offense not to carry ID in the state of New York. The officer retrieved my wallet, and the questions started again. "Where were you coming from this morning?"

"My girlfriend's apartment," I answered.

"Where were you going to?" he asked.

Not thinking straight, I said, "To the Bronx to visit friends."

"But the train was going downtown, not uptown to the Bronx." I was quiet.

"Why were you in such a rush?" he asked. I didn't answer this, but he continued with the questions. "What are you doing in work clothes? There's something not right here. What's your name and address?" As he was questioning me, he pulled out my Drogheda Garda ID—the look on his face was one of complete confusion. "Where is this place?" What are you doing in the state of New York?" he asked.

I said I was on holiday.

"Why are you wearing work clothes with a change of clothes in this bag?" he asked. I replied that I had been doing a bit of painting for my girlfriend.

"You're coming with me. You're not telling the truth. I don't believe you," replied the cop.

I was so afraid. He gave the other officers in the police car a nod, and they got out of the car. *I'm in trouble—I'm going down for this.* It was never my intention to break the law. This was not how my day was meant to end up!

As the cop continued to pull my wallet apart, the NYC PBA World Trade Center Card that my friend John had given me fell out onto the street, and the cop picked it up. He went totally crazy with me, shouting at me and asking where I had gotten the card. He then started accusing me of stealing it.

"I didn't steal the card," I said.

"Shut your mouth, you thief! You are going to be spending some time behind bars. I will make sure you get done for this," he shouted at me.

In my head, I was asking for help. *Please, something or somebody, help me.*

Then I heard the same soft voice in my mind saying, "Tell him who gave you the card." I trusted the guidance and said to him, "I got the card from my cousin, John. He's a transit police detective."

"Oh, did you now? What station does this *John* guy work from?" he asked.

"He doesn't work from a station. He works from an office," I replied, remembering that John had told me to say this if I ever got stopped. I asked the cop to call John, saying that he would explain this and confirm who I was. So the cop rang central station to get transferred to John's number. I could hear the phone ringing, but there was no answer.

He looked at me, and I thought he was starting to understand. He knew I was an illegal! I begged him to call him once more.

"Okay, one more time," the cop agreed. "But if I don't get an answer, you are coming with me." I heard the phone ringing one last time. My heart was pounding. *Please answer, John.* Then I heard John's voice. He answered the phone. Thank God!

The cop started asking John lots of questions. John confirmed I was his cousin and that he had given me the NYC PBA card. The cop apologized to me and said, "You are lucky you know John. You do understand why I arrested you, right?"

I apologized and said I had never meant to break the law. With that, he removed the handcuffs from my wrists. I was free!

I thanked him for not arresting me. The cop then asked if he could help me in any way. "I'm very late now," I said.

"Let me put you back on the train," he said.

I was finally making my way to work. What a morning! I was so relieved to be on the train again. I felt so alive and grateful to the world. It was like God wanted me to wake up and the universe had my back. It was knocking, trying to point me in the right direction, but first, I had a few more lessons to learn.

When I arrived at work, I couldn't get through security. I stood on the street looking up at the roof, trying to catch the attention of one of the other workers. My boss pulled up in his pickup, stopping beside me. He got out and started shouting at me, "What the hell happened to you? The boys rang me to tell me you didn't show up, so I had to come into the city. You are lucky if I don't fire you!"

I tried to explain everything to him, but he didn't want to know, and for the first time in my life, I didn't really care. I felt so free inside. I didn't care that he would not understand. He handed me a bag with the face masks I'd asked for the previous night. I spent the rest of that day counting my blessings, and although I didn't have the awareness at the time, I was completely living in the moment that day!

But my drama in America wasn't due to end yet. There was more to come.

8

One Bang on the Head Too Many

Heading into the middle of summer brought on hot and humid weather. Kim and I were getting ready for the Fourth of July celebrations—Independence Day. This was my first ever Independence Day celebration, so I was super excited. We decided we would rent a beach house for the holiday.

We packed our bags and headed to the Jersey shore for a few days. Kim had suggested we go early so we could enjoy the beach house before everyone else got there. This was my ideal way to celebrate—the sun, sea, sand, and good company.

When we arrived, Kim sorted the bedrooms so we got the biggest room, which was great! We were ready to party! There was a real buzz about the place. It felt like I was in an amazing place with a really good woman. I was so happy. We spent the next few days on the beach swimming and sunbathing in fabulous weather. Lots of parties were happening nearby, so it was hard to decide which one to go to.

I didn't really mind which party we went to, but Kim did like to have things organized, and since there was such a big group of us, she wanted to make sure that we were all going to the same party.

Independence Day

The Fourth of July, 2002, was the day my life changed forever! It was the day that God surrounded me with the Holy Spirit—what I later called my true awakening.

It was a beautiful, sunny day. Everything was beaming and felt perfect. We spent our day at the beach chatting about the various parties we were considering. One massive party held annually stood out from the rest, and of course, we wanted to attend the go-to party.

We all went out for a meal before the party at an Italian restaurant, the craic was great. We all had a laugh and enjoyed ourselves. I met a lot of Kim's friends for the first time, and as I love meeting new people, this was easy for me, especially with the good old Irish gift of the gab!

We finished our meal and decided that it was time to head to the house party. We stopped off at the liquor store to get some beers. Heineken had just brought out the small cans that looked like a keg of beer, so I bought some. We were all in party mode.

I looked at my watch when we arrived at the party—it was 9:11 p.m. People were everywhere on the street, and taxis were pulling up with more. *Wow, this is amazing,* I thought. We were all very excited and looking forward to a great night. We started to make our way toward this massive beach house.

After entering the front gates of the house, we walked through the crowd and headed for the right side of the building. The weather was warm and sweaty; I was wearing a new pair of jeans that were sticking to me. I opened a can of beer and took a drink to cool myself down a bit. We walked up the side of the house and could hear the music getting louder as we got closer. Then we stepped out to the back of the house where the party was in full swing.

We stood at the right corner of the house, debating on what to do next. Some of the group wanted to go to the beach, but Kim and I decided to go further into the backyard, which meant we had to walk under a wooden deck. The deck was roughly twenty by twenty feet, and a lot of people were dancing under it.

We pushed our way through the crowd, very close to the back of the house. I remember looking through a window as we passed by and saw people dancing in the house; it felt like I was looking at two different worlds. People were also partying on the deck above us.

I was really in the moment, soaked up with atmosphere and music. I was walking behind Kim, holding her hand as we pushed our way through the crowd. The beats from the speakers were pumping. I remember thinking, *I feel so tall.*

Everyone was dancing to the music, and Kim turned around to me and said, "I love this song." No sooner were the words out of her mouth than I heard a loud crack, followed by an unmerciful bang on my head. I was knocked unconscious. I was gone.

I was surrounded by a beautiful and calming white light. I knew I wasn't in my body. I started to come back, slowly, and my senses were being reawakened. I couldn't see anything. It was total darkness. The first thing that I heard was people screaming, crying for help.

"Help me! I'm trapped!" echoed loudly. I was confused and didn't know what had just happened. My hearing was affected—it sounded like I was stuck in a tunnel. One minute the voices sounded close up, and the next minute they sounded far away. This created even more confusion for me as I struggled to understand what had just happened.

I was pinned to the ground lying face down, with Kim's legs partially under me. I needed to see if Kim was okay. I reached over and put my hand on her back to see if she was breathing. I could feel her back rising and falling. At least she was alive. I told her not to move and that everything was going to be okay.

People were still screaming, crying, and shouting for help. All of a sudden I felt so calm, which was a surreal feeling in the middle of the mayhem. I didn't know at this point that this would be a major part of my true awakening. This would be the starting point of my spiritual journey, with God reentering my life. But I still wasn't in tune.

I couldn't take a full breath. Everything was still in darkness, and I was breathing in lots of dust. I heard people moving things; it felt like there were things being lifted. I could hear people saying, "Lift, lift." I prayed to God that Kim and I would be okay. Then I saw light coming through the gap that the people had cleared. My eyes tried to adjust to the bright light.

The gap was just big enough for one person to fit through, so I pulled Kim back and pushed her out through the gap. I then followed, feeling my way out. I came across a pair of shoes, which I picked up and took with me. I was in deep shock and injured.

My eyes were still adjusting to the light when I got out, but I could see many, many people lying on the ground. Everyone was in a state of panic. People were being treated by both partygoers and the emergency personnel. People kept coming over to me to ask if I was okay.

"Yes," I replied, "I'm fine, but what exactly happened?"

No one was exactly sure what had happened. From what I could make out, the deck had given way and collapsed, coming down on top of us. Thirty-three people were trapped and injured, but there were no fatalities; we had been blessed.

I couldn't feel any pain. I just walked around dazed and confused. Amazingly, the two cans of beer in my pockets had survived the accident, but they were causing me great discomfort. I tried to get them out of my pockets, but it wasn't an easy task. They were wedged in there. Eventually, I got them both free.

I wandered around with the pair of shoes asking if anyone had lost them. I was interrupted by one of Kim's best friends, who came over to see if I was okay. "Kim is over there. You need to go the hospital," he suggested.

I thought I was okay, but he could clearly see the full extent of my injuries. I ignored Kim's friend's advice because

I was too preoccupied with my irrational thoughts of being illegal. *What if I get caught?* I was in a state of complete and utter fear.

The thoughts that had come to me that day in the subway began to resurface. *Oh, my God, what about all my stuff at my apartment? My friends, Kim, and the life I've made here? I don't want to go home.* I heard Kim's friend speaking in the background still. I could see his lips moving, but all I could think about was running away.

I was looking at the beach and planning my escape route. "Listen, I'm not legal here," I told Kim's friend. "Please don't say anything. I have to get out of here. If I'm caught, I will be deported."

He didn't seem shocked at my revelation. "Don't worry, Robbie. You will be fine," he said reassuringly.

"No, I really have to go," I insisted.

His voice got louder. "You have to go to the hospital! You're injured!" I asked him to meet me a couple of miles down the beach. "What about Kim?" he asked with concern.

"Tell her I'll be fine." I wasn't thinking straight; the fear of getting caught was so overwhelming. All I could think about was getting away.

As I made my way toward the beach, out of nowhere a cop stepped out in front of me. "Hey, where are you going?" he asked. "You're injured."

I was panicking inside, thinking, *I'm caught now. Oh, no, I'm caught. What am I going to do?*

"What's your name and address? Have you got any ID on you?" he asked.

I said I had no ID on me even though my passport was in my back pocket.

"What's your name?" he asked again. I didn't want to give him my name, so I made up a fake name and address. He wrote down the fake details in his book. He then shouted over to a firefighter, "This guy needs to go to the hospital!"

The firefighter walked me over to a stretcher. I looked over my shoulder and saw the possibility of freedom slipping away from me. I was still holding the pair of shoes in my hand. I saw Kim, so I decided to get up and go over to her. I told her that I needed to get away, that she should take my passport and I would get it later. She was crying, pleading for me to go to the hospital, but because I was in so much shock, I didn't realize the extent of Kim's injuries or mine.

I started asking random girls, "Did you lose your shoes?" when I looked at Kim and noticed that she was not wearing any shoes. I looked up and, all of a sudden, for the first time, I saw the full extent of Kim's injuries. Her face was covered in blood. That's when the shock really hit me.

I collapsed to the ground. I was in so much pain. Kim's friends helped me to the step. I was really hurt. I tried to stand up, but I couldn't walk. My foot was badly injured, along with my neck and back. I had a massive cut down my back and a graze on my knee. I started to hop toward the beach. I could see people staring at me with looks of horror on their faces. Out of nowhere, the same cop who had stopped me earlier stepped out in front of me.

He asked me why I hadn't gone to the hospital, and I sensed that he was starting to get suspicious. He took out his book where he had written my fake name and address. "What's your name and address again?" he asked. For the life of me, I couldn't remember the name and address I had given him, so I said my real name and address.

He looked at his book. "That's not the name and address you gave earlier. Who are you here with?" he asked.

"I'm with my girlfriend. She's over there," I replied as I pointed over to Kim. "Listen, I've just had a deck collapse on me. I don't know one day of the week from the next, so I'm sorry if I couldn't remember my name or address." He seemed to accept and understand my reason because he gently took me over to the stretcher Kim was on. He then fetched one for me.

"These guys are in a bad way—get them into the next ambulance," he ordered. Then he moved over to Kim's stretcher. They talked, but I couldn't hear what they were saying. I was trying my best to get Kim's attention to make sure she wouldn't tell him I was illegal. When I heard him saying he was coming with us to the hospital, I automatically thought I was going to be arrested, but thankfully the cop got called to something else. I breathed a sigh of relief as we got wheeled into the back of the ambulance. The doors shut. I was safe.

Kim was really worried about getting to the hospital. I had no medical insurance. In America, people without medical insurance don't get full treatment unless they can pay out of their own pocket. Kim told me to say I was covered on her policy. I reassured her that everything would be okay. When we arrived at the emergency room, we each got taken to different parts of the building. The doctor sent me for some X-rays and a scan. When the nurse asked me for my insurance details, I gave her Kim's policy information, but the nurse then confirmed what we already knew—I wasn't covered. Therefore, I didn't receive full treatment.

The nurses were getting a big kick out my Irish accent. It felt like I was the first Irish person they had ever met. To pass the time, I watched the TV in my room. One of the nurses came in all excited, telling me I was famous. Our accident was headline news on the local news channel.

We spent six to eight hours in the hospital. They bandaged me up, gave me some painkillers, and discharged me. What a way to spend the Fourth of July!

> *Let your heart not be troubled, neither let
> it be afraid. (John 14:27 KJV)*

The Road to Recovery: On a Path
Toward My Darkest Point

Kim's parents came for us and took us to their home by the lake to recover. I was in a bad way. My whole body felt broken, but more than this, my spirit was broken. I could have been killed in the accident. I wondered if this was all part of God's big plan for me.

This was not the first time in my life when my body had been broken and felt pain, but it was most certainly a pinnacle, and my soul felt broken. Although I would later call this my true awakening, it was the beginning of a slippery slope to a very dark point in my life. I was in this internal battle trying to heal and a million miles from knowing how to love myself. This demon had a hold of my heart, it was in my mind, and the thoughts to end my life surfaced again. I felt like I was slowly losing myself, and the accident changed something deep within me. I was screaming for help, but I couldn't get the words out of my mouth. As much as I was grateful for being at Kim's parents' house and for their kindness, I found it difficult to accept this help. This demon they call pride got in my way. I would later find—after I met my guardian angel—that pride had another name. It was the ego mind, the mind of delusion.

Over the next few days, while recovering, the pain was still really intense. Although Kim's injuries were bad, she was mobile. I, however, couldn't move and spent most days in bed, giving me a lot of time to think. My thoughts went deep. I thought a lot about my family, who at this point were unaware of the accident.

After a few days, I decided to phone home and tell them. They didn't realize how bad the accident was because I completely played it down, saying everything was okay. I didn't want to worry them.

Kim's parents encouraged us to ring a lawyer to look into the case, assessing cause for compensation and medical cover. I hadn't told them at that point that I was illegal. It was hard for me to lie to them because I had so much respect for them. Kim wasn't telling them the truth either. I really thought that if they knew I had overstayed my visa, they would not accept me. Not being accepted, or the feeling of rejection, sat in a dark place for me. I had deep-rooted issues that tied in with these subjects, but this was not the time for me to have full understanding of this part of my life.

As the week passed, I was able to move about a little more, but it was still a great struggle. Kim was thinking about going back to work, but I was still not well enough to go back to my apartment in the Bronx. We all sat down for our dinner one evening, and the conversation about seeing a lawyer came up again. "I will wait until I get back to the Bronx and then ring," I told them.

Kim's dad said, "Here's a number a friend gave me. Give him a ring." I went really red in the face with embarrassment, and both of her parents disclosed to me that they knew. "We know, Robbie. It's okay. We have known for a while that you're not legal. Don't worry."

I soon decided that I was well enough to go back to my apartment. My sister had been planning a trip to visit me all year, and I didn't want to let her down. Kim tried to persuade me to stay a bit longer because she felt I wasn't well enough to go back to living on my own. I thought I was fine, or at least I pretended to be fine. I reassured Kim that my friend Neala would be at my place. What I didn't disclose was that Neala was due to go home to Ireland for a trip within the next week or so. I felt I had to stand on my own two feet again. So Kim and I made our way back to the city, and from there I went back to my apartment in the Bronx.

I kept thinking about what Kim's father had said to me about legal advice, and I phoned Kim to discuss. She felt I should seek advice, so I decided to go to the local Irish center and ask for some. I spoke with a woman in the center who gave me the name of an Irish lawyer, and I called him to discuss my case. He felt I had a strong case for compensation but was unsure about how my legal status would affect my case. The lawyer set me up with a specialist doctor in the city, and I finally started to get some proper medical treatment.

I would travel into the city every day to receive my treatments. As I was no longer able to work, my money was slowly running out. Even paying for the subway into the city most days was starting to get difficult. I began to feel trapped, but my pride wouldn't allow me to ask for help. So I didn't eat as much and didn't buy the painkillers I was being prescribed. I was on a slippery slope.

Making my way around was challenging, and the heat didn't help. I hobbled about in my neck collar and back brace, using my crutches to aid me. The one positive thing I had to look forward to was my sister coming to visit. She would be with me for my birthday. I was delighted. I wanted her to have the best time ever.

I decided to save what little money I had for my sister's trip. I literally lived on bread and water for a week until she arrived. That was the toughest week ever as my thoughts turned darker. I was trying hard to block them. It felt like I was in a real battle, looking for some slight glimmer of light at the end of an eternally dark tunnel. This deep and dark depression began to seep in. And what I failed to realize at this point was that my mental health was in a terrible place.

But isn't that something we all do—pretend we're fine because we don't want to become someone else's burden? *Life would go on*, I told myself. It always does.

With God all things are possible.
(Matthew 19:26 KJV)

9

Putting on a Brave Face

My sister Vicky and her boyfriend were arriving soon for their vacation. Even though I was still in a lot of pain, I wanted to show her I was living the dream. I had arranged to meet her in a bar in the city, figuring that would be easier than taking the longer journey to the Bronx. Plus, I thought Manhattan would be a nice way for them to start their holiday.

I made my way to the bar and hung around, waiting for them to arrive. I gave the bartender the details of their flight so that she could check on its status, and she confirmed that the flight from Dublin had landed on schedule. I enjoyed a beer while waiting for them to arrive. An hour passed without any sign of my sister and her boyfriend. I asked the bartender to double check, but she said the flight had definitely landed.

I called my mom again to make sure they had caught their flight, and she assured me that they had. They were now an hour and a half late. I was starting to worry, so I decided to have a look out on the street. *Which way do I go—left or right?* A strong sense came over me: I needed to go left. I trusted my gut and went left. I walked to the end of the block, where I again had to make a choice—left or right?

As I stood at the corner of this block, looking onto an avenue, I felt a strong urge to go right. I walked for about five minutes, crossing about eight blocks, and decided to stop. I thought, *How am I going to find my sister in the middle of New York?*

I was getting concerned at this point. I was considering turning back when something inside stopped me. I looked across the street, and in the distance I saw my sister's long blond hair. I smiled. *Thank God. They have arrived.*

I started whistling as loud as I could and waving my hands in the air. She turned around, waved back, and started making her way toward me. I asked her what had happened, and she said they had given the taxi driver the address for the bar but he drove around in circles saying he couldn't find it. Finally, the taxi driver got frustrated and dumped them both at this corner. Vicky had stood on the side of the street thinking she would not get to see me and would end up spending the whole trip to New York in a hotel.

It was so good to see her. It took the whole focus off my accident and injuries. My sister, being my sister, wanted to know all the details. She was also excited to meet Kim.

Vicky's holiday had officially started. I was so happy. We all went back inside the bar, where the craic was great. The beer was flowing. Vicky couldn't believe that I knew so many people. Nearly every person who walked through the doors of the bar greeted me by name. She was having a good old laugh, saying it was just like I was back home in Drogheda.

Before we knew it, the clock said 9:00 p.m. We were having such a good time that we hadn't noticed the hours pass by. We were all a little tipsy at this stage, so I asked Vicky if she would like to get a taxi home, which would take about fifty minutes, or take the subway so she could see Harlem, Yankee Stadium, and how beautiful the city looked at night.

She looked at me and said, "Whichever you think is best, Robbie. You know the city better than we do!" I suggested the subway. It took a bit longer, but it threw us right into the middle of the Manhattan madness. *Famous last words …*

It Was Like the Scene from the Movie *Ghost*

I told my sister the do's and don'ts of traveling on the subway: "If you make any eye contact, don't stare—look away. When we get down onto the platform, make sure you stand back from the edge of the line."

She had enough luggage to last two months. "What did you pack, Vicky—your entire wardrobe?" I asked.

She laughed and said, "That's to carry some extra clothes on the way home. This is bargain city!"

I laughed to myself, thinking, *With all these bags she must be planning to bring the whole of Fifth Avenue home with her. Typical Irish.*

We were getting close to the subway station, and Vicky was admiring the height of all the buildings. I joked with her, "Don't look up to long. If the wind changes, you will end up stuck that way."

When we arrived at the station, I saw that Vicky was a little apprehensive. I reassured her that we would be fine and continued to crack the jokes.

Our train arrived. We found a seat for the three of us together right inside the door, the closest seat to the adjoining carriage. I was on the right-hand side, Vicky was in the middle, and her boyfriend was on the left. It had been a really hot day, so you can imagine the humidity on the subway. To make matters worse, we couldn't feel the air conditioner until the train pulled off. The doors of the subway carriage closed—*ding dong*—and the train started to pick up speed.

The next thing I knew, the door from the adjoining carriage slid open. A black guy about six feet tall and wearing a trench coat buttoned right up to the neck slammed the carriage door closed. I wasn't really paying too much attention to him as I was daydreaming. He took a couple of steps and suddenly stopped, facing my sister. Out of nowhere, he started screaming at her. "Hey, you white slut! You fucking white slut! You love dildos!"

This all happened so fast. I was trying to register what was going on. I looked over to my sister's boyfriend and saw that he had lost all the color in his face and looked like he was frozen in his seat. Vicky was also glued to her seat. I thought, *What the hell is going on here?* Vicky was wearing a V-neck T-shirt and a chain with a crucifix—real bling. It was an eye-catcher. Things were going in slow motion.

The man was still shouting at my sister. "Who do think you are? White bitch, wearing that cross—do you know Jesus is black?" I quickly remembered my uncle telling us a story when we were kids about nearly being mugged on a train. He said he had gotten up and started to act like he was crazy.

Just like clockwork, I began to sense the presence around us, and I heard the voice in my head saying, *Get up. Do something. Your sister needs your help.* So I got up and started screaming and shouting. I slapped myself on the face and acted completely crazy. I screamed, "Come on! I will take you! Pick on me!" I was making all these funny noises while banging my hands on my chest. Well, let me tell you, this guy didn't know what hit him. He had met his match! He must have felt frightened because he suddenly started running through the carriage.

I shouted at him, "Come back here! I will sort you!" When I turned around, I saw that Vicky was having a massive panic attack, and her boyfriend looked like he had just seen a ghost. I asked Vicky if she was okay. Everyone on the train started clapping. They were all happy that I had stood up to this guy. I was just happy that we were all safe.

I had to stay strong for my sister, but let me tell you, my knees were knocking. I spent the rest of the train ride home reassuring Vicky that this was a one-off.

"East 235ᵗʰ Street: Next Stop"

When we arrived in the Bronx, I was still thinking about the events on the subway as well as my situation and questioning them in my mind. It's funny how we mask things when we are screaming inside. I was starting to break down, but I couldn't name or even describe what I felt inside. I was beginning to feel so separated from everything and was losing my faith, but I can't say why. This darkness was around me; it was the beginning of a major turning point in my life.

We arrived at my apartment. I had only one air conditioning unit and the heat was unbearable, so I set it up in my room and let my sister and her boyfriend stay there. I was used to the heat at night so I didn't mind, but I felt for my sister. It must have been some shock to the system, and what an eventful day!

We spent the next few days traveling around the city. I was having great fun showing Vicky all the sights, including the amazing Empire State Building. A friend of a friend worked on the elevators of the building, so we didn't have to get a ticket or queue. Vicky and her boyfriend felt like VIPs; in fact, we all did. This was such a special moment for me.

I was definitely the best tour guide as we visited the different sights. I didn't have much cash, but I kept a brave face because I was always conscious of not letting Vicky down. However, I knew somewhere deep inside she could see me struggle.

We floated around the city, from the Intrepid Warship Museum to Central Park. Vicky really wanted to see Ground Zero. I hadn't been down there in quite a while. She was so eager to cross the walking bridge and get some photos. We went down one morning and, of course, Vicky asked lots of questions, most of which I couldn't answer. I told her that she would see for herself. Many people were visiting and paying their respects, and my heightened sensitivity to things didn't help me. When we arrived at Ground Zero, I could see the shock on Vicky's face. She looked up to the sky all around her and tried to imagine how tall the buildings really were and the sheer terror that came that day.

She told me that on 9/11, Mom and Dad and all the family were so worried about me. Vicky said, "I now understand what you experienced. It must have been awful." She turned to me and looked right into my eyes. "Are you sure you're okay?"

10

Living It Up in the Big Apple

My birthday was coming up, and I wanted to celebrate while Vicky was with me. Kim had arranged for us to go to this amazing restaurant. She was so kind and thoughtful, always thinking of and doing for others. We all got dressed up and hit the big bright lights of the city; everyone was super excited.

We arrived at the restaurant, and it was so special. The food was great, and the atmosphere felt electric. Kim had really spoiled me. It was so great to be in that special moment with the people I really loved.

When we left the restaurant, Kim had arranged a limousine for us to go downtown to Greenwich Village, and we ended up in a bar called the Red Lion. The drinks flowed, and we sang and danced the night away. The Village is really an amazing place with lots of body piercing and tattoo shops. Someone decided that we should all get something done to mark the occasion.

This sounded like a great idea at the time, and being Irish, we were always up for a laugh and a bit of craic. So we left the pub and looked around in shop windows. We finally found a tattoo shop that looked really good. The next moment, we were inside debating on whether to get a tattoo or a piercing. Vicky, being the most sober, was recording all this on camcorder. Thinking this was all so funny, we decided to get a piercing, and then we had to choose one for one another. Let me tell you—that wasn't a good idea.

I decided that Vicky's boyfriend was to have his lip pierced; it looked really painful. Next it was Kim's turn, and we picked the top part of her ear to be pierced. All Kim could think about was what her parents and people at work would say about it. She screamed the whole time during the piercing. We were all laughing, thinking, *This is such a great idea.*

Then it was my turn, and they decided that I would get the inside of my earlobe (tragus) pierced. Well, that hurt! We heard an American girl screaming "Oh, my God! You guys are crazy!"

Vicky was the only sensible one but made sure to get some good video evidence. We left the tattoo parlor and got back in the limo, headed uptown. I asked the driver to open the sunroof so we could stand up, look out, and scream our heads off just like the movie scene in *Big*. It was the best night ever. We were all pretty merry, so we went back to Kim's apartment and slept.

Sore Heads and Ears

When I woke the next morning, I had a really sore head. As I lifted my head from the pillow, I felt my ear throbbing. It was so sore, and just for a brief moment, I couldn't remember getting my ear pierced. Kim was the same. We looked at each other in disbelief. We both had headaches, but to top it off our ears were sore too.

I got up and woke Vicky up, and we sat in Kim's apartment that morning. All Kim could think about was work and her parents, but it had all been fun at the time. We had the weirdest breakfast ever that morning. I had been telling Vicky about this Mexican restaurant that we ordered from all the time, and it didn't matter what time you ordered—day or night—they were open and delivered. So it was burritos and salad bowls for breakfast.

I know it doesn't sound nice, but in that moment I was so happy. All the thoughts and pain were gone, and I just loved having my sister to visit.

11

The Dark Soul of the Night

In the back of my mind I knew how much Vicky was helping me while she was with me, and I was starting to feel guilty that she was using some of her vacation money on me. This was when I started to really turn from my light, and it's when the dark soul of the night started to creep in.

At this point I felt like I had nothing, and it was so hard not to listen to the voice in my head as it talked to me. I tried to block it out, but I could feel it slowly taking hold of my positive thoughts and replacing them with thoughts of no self-worth. I was hiding this from Kim and especially Vicky, as she too was so sensitive and would notice that there was something wrong.

Why could I not ask for help?

At this time I was so lost; I realize now that I was suffering from post-traumatic stress disorder. All I knew was that the accident that could have killed me might as well have because I was now facing this terrible inner demon. My mental health was at its most volatile. I didn't know who I was, and I didn't have the coping mechanisms to move forward. The walls were closing in. If I kept smiling, no one would see through me. I was so afraid that people might see my pain.

I was extremely hard on myself. I didn't want to fail. This made me even more determined not to break down and ask Kim or Vicky for help.

I would find out later that this was teaching me one of the most valuable lessons in my life.

Only Through My Darkness Could I Find My Light!

The morning I had been dreading had arrived: Vicky was going home to Ireland. As she packed up her things, we chatted and she said to me, "Why don't you come home, Robert? There is no shame. We all think you have done well. Things are too hard for you here with your injuries. You can't work. What are you going to do for money?"

"I will find something," I replied. I felt I had no life back in Ireland and that if I went back I would probably start walking in my old shoes. I didn't want to go back to that part of my life. I knew then and there that I should have said yes, but the words just wouldn't come. I had too much pride, preventing me from making the right choice.

Vicky cried. "We all love you. Please come back home. Please come home." We both cried. It hurt so bad. I looked at Vicky, but I couldn't make the choice. It was like Vicky knew what was happening but didn't know how to help. She gave me the last of her vacation money and said, "You will need this more than me." I had a lump in my throat. The taxi was on its way, and my feelings and emotions were all over the place. I was trying to be strong so I wouldn't worry Vicky and in turn worry my family.

The taxi arrived, and it was time to say goodbye. I said to Vicky, "Will you tell everyone at home I love them so much?" We carried the luggage to the taxi, and Vicky asked if I would be okay. I replied, "I will be fine. Don't you be worrying. I will call down to see Kim later." I said this as a way of doing the big brother thing, and I also didn't want to send any smoke signals home. I didn't want them to think something was wrong.

We said our goodbyes as Vicky got into the taxi, and I had only a minute or two before they left. I was saying goodbye, but in my head what I was really saying was, *Please take me home.*

Vicky said to me again, "Come home. You won't be a failure."

I closed the door of the taxi and stepped back onto the sidewalk, and as the taxi started pulling away, I looked into my sister's eyes. *Please don't go!* I thought. Something snapped inside me. I thought that this would be the last time I would ever see her. The dark soul of night had its grip on me.

The taxi turned the corner, and they were gone. I had never felt so alone in my life. That day I felt so separate from everything, and as I looked out into the world, all I could feel was my darkness. *Why did I not just go home?* I went back into the apartment crying, like a lost sheep looking for its shepherd. The dark soul of the night

97

would present itself this day. It spoke to me: "You are not strong. You're a failure. You're worthless. You are not loved."

Can you imagine what I was going through? I had no answers for this. It was like a black cloud had come over me. I could see no light, only my darkness. I had no understanding of love at this point, no understanding of forgiveness. I was thinking of ending my life.

I felt worthless, and the dark soul made sure that it suppressed and diminished any light that I had. I had hit an all-time low and just couldn't see my way out. I always say that, at this point in my life, all I had left in my soul as it cried out for help was one particle of light—the rest was surrounded by darkness. I wanted to die that day, and those emotions were coming from a horrible, dark place. I hated myself and felt that my life was meaningless. I didn't have the strength to get away as it called to me, "Take your own life. You are unloved. You have failed."

I stayed in my bedroom, still crying. I had a little notice board with some personal items on it. Underneath the notice board, pinned to the wall, I had displayed something my mother had painted for me before I left for America. It was a painting of Jesus Christ's hands. It meant so much to me, but because I was so disconnected at this point, I couldn't see its true value.

My mother had said that the painting would protect me and watch over me—keep me close to Jesus Christ. I looked at it and tried to feel this, but I felt no connection. It was like something had crept in and taken it all from me.

I was angry. I was thinking of my brothers, Joe and Jason; my sister, Vicky; and my mom and dad. I thought of them the whole time I was starting to contemplate taking my life. My aim was to do it so I wouldn't hurt anymore and so I could be free of all the things that were in my head, never once thinking that I was loved. I wasn't intending to hurt anyone.

I also had my uncle Brian and aunt Tammy's phone number on this board. They lived in Boston and we had just been to visit them for a few days. They had given me their number and said that if I ever needed them, just call. I went to bed early that night feeling very depressed, crying myself to sleep. I spent the next day or two in a very dark place. Kim phoned me and asked why I hadn't been in touch. I lied and said that I was busy. She asked if I was okay and said that I didn't sound like I was in a good place. I smoothed it over by saying I was just sad that Vicky had gone and felt a bit lonely.

Kim invited me to come and stay with her in the city for a couple of days. I told her I would come over and stay at the weekend.

Poor Kim had no idea I was in so much pain. And to top it off, I felt so guilty about lying to her, saying I was fine. This was out of character for me. I was always such a straight-up guy. At the end of the phone call, Kim told me she loved me, and I said, "I will see you later."

There will never be a single soul that the love of God will not instill with Hope, as God beckons us toward the light, at every single moment in darkness & light.

Every soul carries the light of God within them.

A Lightless Tunnel: Consumed by The Darkness

I made the decision to end my life.

How did I end up at this point? I had come to America to create the perfect life, to prove to myself that I could make a difference, and to be the person I felt I was somewhere deep inside. I wanted to get away from all the hurt and pain of a childhood for which I had no answers. This was the land where dreams could come true, the land of opportunity, but mine were far removed from that reality.

I took the money Vicky had given me and went to the local deli. I bought alcohol and lots of tablets. The guy behind the counter knew me well because I went into that deli all the time. He looked at me as if to say, *What the hell is he doing*? But he never said anything.

I was focused at this point. I had tunnel vision, and the tunnel I was looking down had no light at the end of it. I went back to the apartment and started to drink, and as I spent the day drinking, I took all of the photos I had with me and began looking through them. I was in a battle with myself. My will to die was so strong that it dampened the sounds of reason telling me not to go through with it. I got a pen and paper and started to write a final letter to my family, telling them how sorry I was and how much I loved them. Writing was never my best skill. I am left-handed, and in school this was nearly beaten out of me.

As I wrote, I started making some spelling mistakes, so I crumpled up that one and a few more after that. My soul cried out that night, and it was heard in the heavens.

I was getting drunk, which made all my feelings more heightened and amplified. I was getting close to taking the tablets; I opened the bottle of spirits as I was finishing my letter. *Why am I so sad? How did my life end up here?* I was so angry with God. I had no faith. *Why does there have to be so much pain in this world?* Everywhere I looked, all I saw was people struggling and suffering.

I was in total despair at that moment, choosing to end it all. I blamed the world because my understanding at that time had no other option; there was no turning back.

I opened the tablets and took them one at a time, drinking to wash them down. I started to fold up all my stuff on the bed. In the middle of my madness, while the tears were dripping down my face, I thought, *What am I doing?* But the dark soul was with me. I started to feel the effects, and I shouted out, "Sorry, Mom and Dad! Please forgive me."

The pain I felt was unreal. Even to this day I can't describe it, and I will never find the words to express it. I had the cordless phone in my room, so I took it to the holder in the living room, staggered back to my room, and locked the door. I was starting to feel weak and slipping in and out of consciousness. I swallowed the last of the tablets.

My life was starting to flash in front of me. I saw different memories from my life. I was delirious with so much drink and so many tablets.

What have I done? I looked at my mom's painting on the wall, and I can still remember my last thoughts as I called out, "Please save me! Please forgive me, for I know not what I do."

101

Divine Intervention

I came around to find that I was lying on the floor, and I heard a voice. The phone was in my hand; on the other end were Brian and Tammy saying, "Hang in there. We love you." I felt pretty messed up, but I had survived. They kept me on the phone talking. My room was full of light, the Holy Spirit, like the sun; God heard my cry for help. It was blindingly bright, but it was the middle of the night.

I was trying to figure out how the phone had gotten into my hand. How had I rung Brian and Tammy? I felt sick and was still pretty out of it. I looked over to the wall and saw that my mother's painting was gone. I was confused. I was talking to Brian and could tell that he was really worried. I wasn't making much sense. I asked, "How did you ring me?"

He replied, "I didn't. The phone rang, and it was you on the other end. Are you okay? Hang in there. I will come for you." He and Tammy stayed on the phone for a good while until I started making more sense. Oh, I felt like crap! *What have I done?* I had tried to kill myself and was lucky to survive, but somehow I felt like a total failure.

I still couldn't understand how the phone had gotten into my room. As I became more aware, the brightness in the room started to recede. The feeling in the room was so strong. It was the same presence I had felt as a child and at other times leading up to this moment, but it was a million times stronger. I looked around the room for my mom's painting, but I couldn't see it. I thought, *I put a pin in it so it wouldn't come off the wall. Where could it be?* I went to my bedroom door and found that it was still locked. I opened the door and went to the kitchen to get some water. I was very badly dehydrated.

When I passed the phone holder, I saw my mom's painting. It was there, right next to the holder. I couldn't believe it. *What on earth is going on?*

I'd survived at the hand of God. Jesus Christ's love saved me from this demon and my mom's painting kept my connection to God open. This was a major part of my awakening, preparing me for Gods plan. Brian was on his way from Boston to see me. I was in such a dark place but really grateful to be alive. I felt very guilty, though, and I wasn't sure how Brian would react when he arrived. As I waited for him, I kept thinking about the miracle of how Mom's painting had ended up in the living room and the phone had ended up in my room.

The time was coming when I would ask the biggest question of my whole life, about all the things I had sensed as a child, young adult, and now, in my early twenties. Yet I was still very much in denial, so I had a little bit more to go. Things were going to change from this day forward; it was never going to be same. From this moment, my life started, and my soul's purpose and true journey began.

Brian arrived the next morning. I had always looked up to him—a very wise soul. I put on a brave face, but there was no doubt he could see straight through me. He never once said anything about it. He showed nothing but unconditional love and understanding, and he asked me to come back to Boston with him. I had no intention of going, but he convinced me to come and stay for a few weeks until I felt better.

All I could think about was Kim. Brian said, "Give her a call and let her know that you're staying with us." I did but didn't tell her why, and she was a little pissed off with me. I never told her what had happened, that I had tried to take my own life. As I spoke to her on the phone, I felt so sad. It was like a major shift; a disconnection had happened within me. I felt like I had let her down completely after everything she had helped me with.

I remembered all the good and happy times with her and the love she had for me. But I still didn't know how to love myself. I was broken and trying to find the man I was within.

As I packed my stuff for my journey to Boston, Brian was so kind, compassionate, and understanding. He shone so much light on me. Leaving New York, I was thinking the whole time, *I will be back. I'm only going to stay up with Brian and Tammy for a few weeks until I feel better.*

Little did I know!

12

The Awakening: The Light of God Will Always Find You

Our journey was going to take five hours, and I worried about what we would talk about during this time. I hoped Brian wouldn't ask me too much about what I had just tried and why I had tried it.

On our way, we spoke about many things—about my mom and my childhood. We also spoke about God and spirituality. I totally closed down and went into judgment mode. I let the voice of everyone else's dogma wash over me: my aunt and uncle were Bible bashers. Well, they weren't going to convert me. *I'm just staying a couple of weeks and getting the hell out of Dodge City and back to New York.*

This may sound ungrateful, but it was just where I was at this time. What my journey would soon reveal to me was that they were both very spiritual people, with great understanding and wisdom, but my fear wouldn't let me see it at that time. I am sure we have all done this before—listened to someone else's view and created a judgment based on it. I was starting to learn a little about love, compassion, and forgiveness but in a really subtle way. Brian kept shining his light.

We arrived in Boston, and it was great to see Tammy and the kids. They gave me a really warm welcome and had a room ready for me in the basement. I was happy to be with family, but they were different from any people I had ever been with before, and trying to find the words to describe it would do it no justice. They were just so in tune with God, the world, and life. I had only just arrived and could already sense this. It was very different from my family home. This house was relaxed and had such loving vibes.

I spent my first week sleeping.

I was in a black depression, so I found it hard to get motivated. But Brian and Tammy were constantly supportive. I felt safe but still had a lot of stuff going on in my mind, plus I was beginning to experience paranormal activity. This was a really confusing time for me. It seemed to happen mostly when I was in my room, and I thought I was losing my mind. I didn't know what to say to Brian and Tammy, even though I knew they would totally understand.

My belongings were being moved in my bedroom, then they would go missing, and finally they would turn up exactly where I had left them. I was starting to see stuff moving around my room. I'd light a candle, and it would levitate across the room. I started to wonder if I was going crazy! I thought that if I said anything to Brian and

Tammy, I would end up in a psychiatric ward, and the fact that I had tried to take my own life would make for a strong case. I kept it zipped.

In the evenings, I would eat with the family. Brian began to speak to me about how he had found it hard to cope after his father (my grandfather) died. He explained that he went to see a man who could communicate with the dead. I really trusted him; if anyone else had said this to me, I would have closed down. But I knew Brian would not tell a lie. He had a way of making me feel at ease, never pushing his beliefs on me.

I didn't tell them I was experiencing all this crazy stuff, like the bedside lamp going on or off when it was unplugged. I was still trying to cope with my life and past, and as we spoke, he had this amazing ability to get into my past and talk about it.

This was something I had never done in my life up to this point. In my childhood home, we hadn't spoken about problems. This was all new to me. I found it really hard, but as I say, I trusted him, and the process did make my life a lot easier.

After that first week of sleeping and resting, I did start to come out of my cave. For the first time in my whole life, I was facing Robbie. I was trying to understand how complex I was as a person, and talking about things I had buried inside me for most of my life really helped. My childhood came up a lot, but I was not ready to face those demons. The process had to be done one step at a time. My wounds were deep, but the love I was shown was something I will always be grateful for.

Tammy's grandmother had a swimming pool, so we would go there most evenings to barbecue and swim. This helped me with my injuries and recovery, and it was great to spend time with Tammy's family. Her grandmother was the most straight-talking lady I have ever met and had a sense of humor like I had never witnessed. There was lots of laughter, and laughter is definitely good soul therapy.

I thought often of home and my mom. I was feeling homesick, but I didn't want to live at home. Funny, I know—I just worried about my mom because I knew she was finding it hard to cope as she was still mourning the death of my grandfather.

I phoned home to speak with my family and tell them I was living with Brian and Tammy for a short while. I didn't phone home often, as I didn't want to encourage any late-night phone calls after my mom got home from a night out, usually fairly upset. It's not that I didn't want to speak to her, but if I took a late-night phone call, I had to listen to all the hurt and pain that she was still stuck in. It was like she couldn't move on. I felt that she was in such a dark place at the time. I was also in a dark place, and I found it hard to cope with myself, much less with clashing with Mom. It was great to chat, though.

I hadn't spoken to Kim since I left Manhattan and felt a massive block regarding her. *What is wrong with me?* I couldn't cope. I was meant to call Kim, but I kept putting it off. I procrastinated even though, deep down inside, I knew I shouldn't. However, I felt trapped in my emotions. My whole life had just been turned upside down, and it was time to try and find the person I was within. I didn't have the strength to face our relationship.

Brian and Tammy introduced me to a friend named Doug, a painter, and asked him if he would give me a couple of days' work. He told them he would have to look at what jobs were coming up but that he was unsure because I was illegal.

Early one morning, Doug called to say that he had a few days' work for me. He asked if I would be able to start that morning. "Yes. What time should I be ready?" I asked.

"Now," Doug replied.

"What do you mean *now*?" I asked.

"Take a look outside. Can you see a white van?" he replied. I looked out the window and did in fact see a white van. "Well, that's me," he said. When I think back to this, it still makes me laugh. It would be the start of a very interesting relationship.

I put the phone down and rushed to grab some clothes while Tammy packed me some lunch. She was so happy for me.

I went to work that morning with Doug, and the sun was shining. He was very laid back, but what I found funny was that from the moment I got into the van, we connected. The conversation was nice and light. He asked me if I had done any painting before, and I replied, "Honestly, only a little."

"Well, you have come to the right man! I will teach you how to paint—I have thirty years of painting experience. I am going to teach you all I know." Of course I was delighted and thought this was great. I was getting cash in my hand and working outside in the sun.

We arrived at the job, and Doug asked me to set him up and put the sheets on the ground so there wouldn't be any paint spills. I was surprised at the perfectionist that came out in me on my first day with Doug. He instructed me to paint a back wall, and I spent all morning painting that wall. When Doug reappeared to see what I'd done, he was shocked at how long it had taken me. He had painted half the front of the house in the same amount of time!

During our lunch break, Doug asked me lots of questions about my circumstances, like why I was staying with Brian and Tammy and why I was illegal. I changed the subject at every opportunity because I didn't know Doug too well, and I didn't feel comfortable sharing my whole life story with him. I gathered from him that he was on a spiritual journey and had some sort of tragic past, but he wasn't giving too much away about himself either.

When I got in that day from work, Tammy told me that Kim had phoned. She thought I should call her back and let her know I was okay. I was bright red from the sun, but the color didn't take long to drain from me. Inside, I thought, *Robbie, go ring her.* But another other part of me couldn't do it. I didn't know what to say, so I told Tammy I would call that evening. But I didn't. I felt like crap.

I wasn't trying to hurt Kim, and I most certainly didn't want to put myself through any more pain. But I was also in the middle of my madness with numerous things going on around me. I went to bed that night feeling as if God was highlighting things for me.

I didn't sleep well. During the middle of the night I heard the answering machine click on and then my mother's voice as she left a message. It started off light and friendly but quickly deteriorated into a rant. I lay in bed feeling sick in the pit of my stomach. I felt tremendously anxious; it was horrible and reminded me of the feelings I had in my childhood. So I had Kim calling that day and my mom calling that night, and I couldn't answer either.

I woke up the next morning feeling angry with my mom. "Your mom left a message last night," Brian told me.

"I heard her," I replied. He told me it wasn't bad; she was just hurting.

I went to work that day, and Doug knew that something was up with me. I didn't want to speak about my life to him, though, so I masked it off, put my head down, and painted, but for the whole day I was so angry.

Doug started to open up to me, talking about his life. It sounded very similar to mine back when I was drinking and doing drugs. He started preaching to me about the do's and don'ts of life. I have to say—I was so caught up in my own crap that I didn't completely tune in. Lunchtime came and Doug told me he had to go away for an hour. He said, "If I'm not back, just start back to work yourself."

He was gone a good hour and a half, and when he came back he was chatty and looked a lot lighter. I didn't ask what was going on, but I could see the difference in him. He was a real joker and full of joy, and it didn't take long to get me to laugh. We listened to the radio and sang along to the songs. We were like two brothers who had known each other all our lives, even though it had only been a short while.

Over the next couple of days, he disappeared at lunchtime. I took breaks by myself. I will never forget the silence as I spent this time alone. I reflected a lot on trying to kill myself in my apartment and also tried to remember my childhood. I couldn't unlock the answers, and that frustrated me.

Each evening when I came home from work, Tammy would say, "Kim called again." But I just couldn't pick up the phone and call her back, and the longer I left it, the harder it got. I was a man acting like a child, having Tammy make excuses and lie for me. I should have never put her in that position. I didn't have the answers at this time in my life; it would have been a lot easier if I had. It was easier to hide even though I was causing hurt and pain.

At the end of my first week with Doug, he asked me to work with him the following week. I was happy with that. I spent that weekend chilling with Brian and Tammy and the kids. We went to the beach during amazing weather.

On Saturday night, as I lay in bed, I heard the phone ringing upstairs. At that time of the night, who else could it have been? I went up the stairs and answered the phone. The conversation started off okay, but as it continued Mom started ranting again.

I didn't have much patience. I was a hothead, not having enough empathy and compassion for my mom's pain. I felt that I had always listened to the same story, so I was angry.

I asked my mom not to call the house in the middle of the night anymore as it wasn't fair for everyone else in the house—the kids were sleeping, after all. Mom went straight into defense mode; it was like I had shown a red rag to a bull. She said it was her brother's home, that she would ring whenever she felt like it, and that I was her son and she would speak to me in whatever way she wanted. We argued for a few moments, then I hung up and disconnected the phone. It was all I could do so as not to wake everyone in the house up with our fighting.

This was a really hard time for me. My whole life was upside down, and I felt hurt and confused. I loved my mom and didn't want to be fighting with her. The anxious feelings were back.

When I got up the next day, I knew Brian and Tammy had heard the conversation. Brian was understanding and reassured me that things would be okay. I spent that day in my room feeling depressed, and now I felt this dread every time the phone rang. Was it going to be Mom or Kim? Neither one could I face.

On Monday morning, I felt like crap. The black depression was hanging over me again. Doug arrived; I could hear him upstairs. I was down in my basement bedroom, and I didn't want to go to work. Tammy called down a couple of times saying that Doug was there. All I wanted to do was get back into bed and feel like crap for the day, but this was not the answer.

Tammy came down and asked if I was okay. I told her I didn't want to go in as I felt crap. She wasn't buying it. It was time for a bit of tough love. "Well you better go up and tell Doug you won't be going in," she told me. I was half expecting her to do it for me, but she said, "No. You're a man, so act like one."

I went up the stairs, and Doug was his usual happy and bright self. "What's up with you?" he asked. "We're going to be late. Come on, get your act together."

I was thinking, *What will I say?*

Before I got a chance to speak, Doug said, "Get your ass out to that van. You started this job with me, and by hell you will finish it. You have two minutes. I will see you at the van."

Tough love, but it motivated me to get ready.

In the van, Doug started to talk about different aspects of his life: his relationship with his parents and how he ended up abusing alcohol and drugs. He had many failed relationships in his life, and it took him many years to find peace. He asked me lots of questions, and I opened up a bit. I told him about different situations I had been in, and he totally understood. I told him about that I had tried to kill myself. He showed so much compassion! Yet again, God brought me just what I needed at that moment.

Doug asked me if I wanted to join him for lunch this particular day. I asked him where he was going. "I go to a meeting every day—an AA meeting. It's for people with drinking problems. There are also people there with drug problems. We meet every day and share our stories. I think it will help you when you hear what other people have been through," Doug suggested.

"How will this help me?" I asked. "I am not an alcoholic."

Admittedly, I was a binge drinker and had taken drugs in the past, so I was curious to learn more about this program. Doug informed me that an alcoholic isn't necessarily someone who drinks every day and night, which I foolishly believed to be true. He explained that an alcoholic could be someone who simply doesn't know how to stop drinking after one drink.

When we arrived at the AA meeting, I was shocked at all the different types of people there. It wasn't at all like what I had visualized. I wasn't paying too much attention to begin with, but when the first person got up to speak, I started to tune in. This person talked about all the pain they had in their life and how they had hit rock bottom and that from there, their life had changed. They also talked about spirituality and God. I wasn't ready to fully accept this, but I was willing to listen.

As the meeting continued over lunch, different people shared—men and women, young and old. At the end I was invited to share my story, but I declined. I didn't feel like I had anything to contribute. But I was surprised at how much happier and better I felt after the meeting—although I struggled with the whole God thing.

Doug was like my mentor. He was really helping me. We spent the next few days going to the AA meetings, and I got a lot from them. When I told Brian and Tammy about the two of us going to the AA meetings, they thought it was amazing. I could really feel myself opening up. I started to notice things more when I was painting, like the sounds in nature. It was like my antenna was starting to receive different stations.

What was really being highlighted for me at these meetings was the argument my mom and I had. I didn't want the disharmony to continue. I confided in Doug about my feelings. "It's funny, Robbie, but God will always give to you a moment to heal at any point" he said. "All you have to do is listen." I was trying to understand this, but it kind of went in one ear and out the other. I felt I was separate from God and struggled with understanding God within myself.

Doug suggested that I speak at the next meeting. With his support, I stood up and spoke for ten minutes. I still don't remember what I said, but it felt great—like the weight of the world had been lifted off my shoulders. My thoughts were of my mom and how much I loved her in that moment. It was a moment of bliss.

When we returned to work that day, I felt like I was floating because I had let go of some of the anger I had been holding onto. What happened next was one of my first experiences of synchronicity. I was up on the ladder painting away with the radio playing on a country station in the background. I was thinking about my mom, apologizing to her in my head. The next thing I heard was the deejay on the radio announcing a song by an Irish pop band called Boyzone—my mom's favorite band.

Freaky, I thought.

Boyzone was never played on this radio station. Then the deejay announced the song he was going to play; it was my mom's favorite.

I nearly fell off the ladder! I screamed at Doug, "Do you hear this song?" He looked at me like I was losing my mind. I couldn't believe that my mom's favorite song was being played on American radio. Holy Moly, was this God's way of saying hello or what?

When things like this happen—and they happen all the time—we really need to be aware of the messages we are receiving. God is always supporting and helping us. It is our job to tune in and listen.

This was my last week working with Doug because he had no more cash jobs. My time with Doug was invaluable, a very important part of my journey.

Come unto me, all you that labor and are
heavy laden, and I will give you rest.
(Matthew 11:28 KJV)

117

13

Light and Shadows

I started to notice shadows and various colors around people. I was living with lots of fear, and when I went to bed at night, sometimes the shadows would appear, some of which didn't feel nice. They would make the hairs on the back of my neck stand on end. The room would get cold. I would close my door because when I looked out into the rest of the basement, I could see where the dark shadows were coming in. It was really weird.

I would hide my head under the blankets and pray that they would go away. It worked. It's funny—I was an adult and for the first time in my life I was sleeping with the light on and hiding under the blankets.

The shadows were like silhouettes, outlines that resembled a human body, but not all of them seemed unfriendly. It was like they had different energies. I was also seeing round balls of light and beautiful, vibrant colors. The balls of light would dance around my room at night.

I also started to see flashes of light around people, like sparkles. *What is going on?* I wondered.

Brian and Tammy had numerous spiritual books, and we had interesting, deep discussions every evening about life and our purpose in it. Tammy suggested that I read one of the books because she felt it would help me. I hadn't confided in Tammy or Brian about my experiences, yet they somehow just knew. They were like my spiritual mentors, helping me, guiding me, and pointing me toward my path.

I still had lots of resistance and questions. I had never really read a book in my life up until this point. It wasn't something I thought I could do because of my negative school experiences. Tammy continued to insist that I read this particular book. "I have the perfect book for you, Robbie," she said. To get her off my back, I took the book and threw it on the floor of my bedroom with no interest whatsoever.

Two steps forward, three steps back.

The Demon Drink Shows Its Face Again

I had made some new friends in the area. Tammy and Brian told me that, even though these guys were nice, they sometimes got into a bit of trouble. "Don't be trying to drink with these guys," Tammy warned. I didn't really listen to her advice, but I would soon learn a lesson very quickly.

We went out on a one-day pub crawl, playing pool and drinking beers. We were having a good time until we got to this one bar. I was feeling tipsy and in hindsight should have called it a day, but one of the guys started drinking whiskey and asked me to have a shot of it with him. When I said no, the slagging and piss-taking started, so I gave in to the peer pressure and began throwing back the shots of whiskey. It started to become a competition to see who could drink the most.

"I thought you Irish could drink," he teased.

Half a bottle of whiskey later, I wasn't making much sense. A guy at the bar asked if we wanted to play a game of pool for money. We had been holding the pool table for a few good games at this point. One of my mates was getting louder by the minute with all the alcohol we had consumed. "Let's play for fifty dollars," the guy said.

I didn't have that kind of money on me, but before I could reply my mate said, "Yeah, we'll play for fifty dollars. We will kick your ass." I started to feel the cold around me; it was a dark feeling, and it scared me.

As we continued to win, potting ball after ball, I could tell that the other two guys were getting angry. I saw very tall, dark shadows hovering around them and did not have a good feeling. I said, "Sure, let's just not play for money. It's only a bit of craic."

The next thing I knew, my mate sunk the winning ball. It was all over. We had won.

Our two opponents were pissed off. I tried to reason with them. I wasn't long about sobering up after that.

"You cheated, and you're going to pay," one of them ranted.

My mate was at the bar and didn't see this happening. I tried desperately to get his attention. It was like I was stuck in a time warp. I tried to reason with the guys, saying I didn't want to fight and we didn't cheat. "What if we give you your money back?" I offered.

"No, we have been waiting for the chance to get you," he snarled. I was apprehensive but was ready to stand up for myself if I needed to. I saw those tall, dark shadows making their way toward me. Suddenly, a bottle flew across the room and smashed beside me. I was in the middle of a bar fight! It was like something out of a John Wayne movie.

The fight began to spread around the bar, with more people getting involved. "The police are on their way!" the bartender shouted. I was in a scuffle when I saw a flash of light by the door. I heard a gentle voice saying, *Leave now.*

I ran out of the bar and down some narrow streets to get away. I could hear the police cars in the distance. I thought, *Feck me, I'm in big trouble.* I noticed a police car heading right for me, so I jumped a fence and started running around the backs of buildings, hopping more fences as I ran.

I ended up on a back street. I ducked behind a wall when I heard a car approaching me, but then I heard my named being called. It was one of my mates from the bar. I got into the back seat, and they covered me with jackets. *What will my aunt and uncle think?* I thought. *I'm not a troublemaker!* I felt sick. "Stop the car! Stop the car!" I shouted. They pulled over, and I vomited out the side of the car.

When we arrived at my aunt and uncle's house, they pulled the car in quickly and let me out before speeding off. I stood at the back door trying to sober up, thinking about what I was going to say if they were still up. I made my way through the door and found that everyone was sleeping.

I got to the door at the top of the basement and noticed a tarot card lying on the floor, which totally freaked me out. When I looked at it, something clicked inside me. It was like a movie in my mind, and I could see everything clearly.

It was dark. It was unimaginable and scared me. I knew these cards represented something evil; I could sense that. I saw myself in the darkest place I had ever imagined. My loved ones were not there; I was alone. It was like God gave me a glimpse of what hell would be, I thought, *Oh, my God, please never send me there.*

I broke down crying. I cried so hard that I began wailing. I woke up everyone in the house. Tammy and Brian came running out of their bedroom to see what on earth was going on.

I wasn't making any sense; the tears dripped down my face. Bless them, they must have really thought that I had lost my mind. All I could do was point at the card and say, "My life, my life."

They got me a cup of coffee. Brian stayed up for a while sharing his words of wisdom with me. He said, "Robbie, drinking will only bring you away from the light that you are. It attracts all the darkness that you are also. You are very special. It's time to become a man and start making the right decisions about your life."

The next day, I felt horrible. I had a hangover from hell and was in a dark place again. At breakfast that morning, I was grumpy with the kids and took my crap out on them, which wasn't very fair as all they showed me was unconditional love. Tammy looked annoyed but didn't say anything. She took the kids and went off for the day. I felt so bad and guilty inside. Brian had some sort of an understanding and went easy on me.

When Tammy came back that evening, she told us there had been a big fight in a bar the previous night in town. *Oh crap.* I piped up and said that it was me—I was there, I was drinking whiskey thinking I could keep up with these guys, but I couldn't. "I'm really sorry for everything," I said. "I didn't mean to cause any trouble. I'm sorry if I was off with the kids. I love them."

"It's okay," Tammy said.

This was a point where I felt loved and knew they really cared for me. I made the decision to stop drinking because, when I drank, I didn't know the cut-off point. Drinking was my sticky plaster; it would not help me to grow and heal.

It was like God was guiding me to stay away from tarot cards. Whatever the tarot card had ignited in me—the movie that played out in my mind that was so dark—I knew that wasn't what I wanted my life to be like. I wanted to explore a happier life and wanted to experience more love.

14

The Book on the Floor Is Calling Me: *Read Me, Robbie. Read Me*

The book Tammy wanted me to read lay on the floor of my bedroom. You'll never guess what happened. The book started to call me. I know this may sound funny or even hard to believe, but you can only imagine what was going through my head!

Every single night I would go to bed, and as I lay down to go sleep, the book would call out, *Read me, Robbie. Read me.* This was yet another moment of craziness. I was fighting against reading it, and yet the magnetism of the book intensified.

One evening, I couldn't block out the sound of the book anymore. The feelings inside me were so strong that I had to see what was in this book. It was the first spiritual book I had ever read. In fact, it was the first *adult* book I had ever read! I picked up the book and opened the first page.

It told the story of a guy who could communicate with the spirit world. As I began to read that night, it felt as if the book related to my life. For the first time, a moment of true awakening took place to answer my many deep questions. It was like I had been looking at my life as a blurry picture, and then it started to become clear, like the darkness had begun to lift.

In that moment, I felt every positive emotion throughout my body. I was buzzing. I was hooked! I read into the early hours of the morning. I was a slow reader, and because this was the first book I was reading all the way through, I needed to read back through certain sections a couple of times until they made sense. After that, I would fall asleep.

I woke the next morning but didn't go up for breakfast. I started reading again. It really felt like it was my life I was reading about. I felt a real connection. *I'm alive!* It was like being awakened from a deep dream. Finally, my life was starting to make sense. This was my first light-bulb moment in quite a while. I couldn't put the book down.

Brian thought I was on hunger strike. I was not one who usually passed on food, so I decided to join them for breakfast, book in hand. When Brian and Tammy saw the book, their faces lit up. They looked so happy. "I see you started reading," Brian said. Deep down inside, the fire within my soul was alight and burning.

I spent the next couple of days immersed in the book, not wanting to put it down. I read from the moment I woke to the moment I fell asleep. Brian and Tammy didn't see much of me during this time. They must have thought I had become a hermit! The writer's experiences described in the book were so similar to mine that it felt as if he had written it especially for me.

All of the things I had experienced and felt as a child, teenager, and young adult were finally making sense. There was a higher reason for this. Because I had never questioned my childhood experiences, my sense of purity prevailed. Then, as a teen, I closed down completely and pushed my emotions away as a coping mechanism. Being a young adult, I was lost in all these other realities of life. I had no understanding or anyone to help me understand.

As I read through the book, it talked about spirits and spirit guides, angels and healing—all the things I had been experiencing. This was the first piece of the jigsaw puzzle of my life.

I decided to clear my bedside locker as I felt the need to put in it the things that meant the most to me. It became like a little altar.

I asked lots of questions in my mind, as you can imagine. I wanted the answers as to why I had always noticed certain things in life. Why was I so sensitive to people, their emotions, and their energy? I wanted to see through the veil of illusion. I was looking for validation.

As the book came to a close, it sparked the biggest question I had ever asked myself. I felt angry and hurt with God and his angels. I need to make this clear. Within myself, I was asking a direct question to God. I needed the answers from him. I was talking to nothing else and no one else but God. The answers I was searching for couldn't come from anywhere else.

God, why have you abandoned me?

This question led me to other thoughts, deeper thoughts. They were like tangents, spreading through my mind as my perceptions developed and grew.

Is this world a big joke? Because if it is, I must be the only one who is not laughing. I must have missed the punchline.

God, I'm so confused and angry. I read this book—it's opened me up and connected some of the dots, yet I feel now I'm losing all faith and can't validate my life. Are you real, God? Please show me a sign.

God, can you hear me? I'm screaming in my mind and from the depths of my soul, begging for an answer. Please show me a sign. I'm looking for evidence. I need it to go on, to give my life worth and meaning. I need it to fill the void, to change it from darkness to light.

On this day, my ongoing conversation with God started. I talked to God and God alone. I asked him questions with every single thought I had and at every single moment. I never stopped asking.

Are you real? If so, show yourself to me. Can you hear me, God?

I screamed with all my hurt at that moment.

Send me a sign. I need a sign. Please, I need something to make this real for me.

With these cries for desperation, my mind began to shift. I began thinking of my relatives, of those who had gone before me. I started asking everyone I could think of in heaven to send me a sign. I asked my grandfather to come through to me and help me. I have to say—this helped me to discipline my mind, like a form of meditation.

When I chatted with Brian and Tammy, in another part of my mind, I asked God questions. My mind never stopped searching for the answers. When I was in my bedroom alone, I spoke out loud until I fell asleep. I was desperate for a validation that would reinstill in my life a sense of purpose and meaning.

At this time, I reflected on many different parts of my life. I did the one thing I have always done to myself— beat myself up. I thought of my family and how much I loved them, yet I looked back on my life at all the disharmony we had experienced. I just wanted to heal this.

Ask, and it shall be given you. (Matthew 7:7 KJV)

Brian helped me find another job, this time in a local service station as a gasoline attendant. It was great because it gave me some independence. The guy who owned the garage was a real nice guy, thank God. I put gas into the cars and looked after the shop.

The weather started to get cold, so I wore my brand new snow gear. Even though there was no snow, it could get windy on the garage forecourt, and when I was doing eight-hour shifts, I could get very cold. The cold made my body feel sore and tired where I had been injured in the Fourth of July accident, but I managed.

I felt settled for the first time in a long time. I felt I belonged somewhere, and my relationship with Brian and Tammy was truly special. They were my spiritual mentors, guiding me to my true path in life.

Brian had gone to see a guy who was a medium, and my grandfather came through to him. Brian felt that seeing this medium would help me tremendously, but I just wasn't ready.

Even though I was going through many experiences, I was still skeptical. All I could think was, *How can he tell me anything about my life?* I wanted God to validate my life. I didn't think a medium could bring me the answers I craved.

15

How I Met My Guardian Angel

November 22, 2002:
The Day God Sent Me My Sign

My guardian angel was a sign from God. This was the day I found my true path in life, the day God gave me back my faith. This time it would be sealed within the very seat of my soul. From this day on, I would never be in a place of fear. The foundation would be set, building the person I was born to be.

I was born to shine, just like you! It is my path in this lifetime to bring the light of unconditional love to the souls that need me to help them, to be of service to the love and light of God.

From darkness to light.

I woke up, and the morning was still. I started my day by asking God to bring me a sign. It was cold outside, so

I put on my snow gear and then went upstairs for some breakfast before my morning shift. I felt happy. The day felt different. I can't explain it.

My aunt Tammy is a great cook and always had something special for my breakfast. She also packed me a lunch every day for work. They really did spoil me. They treated me just like their own kids, only I was a twenty-something-year-old kid! I loved it all the same.

I had started to think about Christmas—it was only around the corner. My thoughts turned to my family. I don't know why, but Christmas wasn't my favorite time of the year. Yet I was looking forward to spending it with Brian and Tammy and their kids.

The gas station where I worked was only a five-minute walk from my home, so I usually left about ten minutes before my shift started. As I finished up my breakfast, the house started to get busy with the kids. My aunt looked after another couple of kids as well, so things were all go for her at this time of the morning. I grabbed my coat and headed out the front door, shouting back to them, "See you later!"

As I walked to work, I thought about my life yet again, wondering if this lost feeling would ever go away. I asked God some of the same questions again: *Where am I going? Are you real? Please tell me. What is my purpose?*

When I arrived at work, my boss had already opened up. He wasn't going to stay for long as he had a busy morning. He gave me my till float for the day and left. The morning was slow, but I didn't mind. I alternated between tending to the pumps and the shop. I was getting used to seeing the familiar faces that stopped for fuel. Most of them were regulars—the garage always seemed to have the best prices around.

When that garage got busy, it was *really* busy. I got good tips, which my boss found funny because it wasn't something people normally did. I didn't complain though! The extra cash came in handy.

The morning was passing by so fast, and I had a good, steady flow coming in and out of the garage. Then out of nowhere, it got very busy. I was run off my feet. My boss came back, which was unusual. He said he was driving by, saw how busy it was, and decided to stop and give me a hand. He took some cash off me as there was no safe to keep it in. I could be carrying a couple of thousand dollars or more at any given time. He hung around for about twenty minutes until things quieted down, and off he went.

The gas pumps were old and dated. If you can imagine, they had three different speeds: five, ten, and fifteen. The fuel would pump faster or slower depending on what speed was set. I would set the pump speed according to the amount of fuel going in so I could keep all the cars moving at a steady pace. I was going full steam ahead.

My ankle and neck were sore from the cold weather. I was soldiering on, though, with a good old, hardworking, Irish spirit! I stood in the center of the island where the pumps were. In the middle of the busyness, a particular car pulled in; I remember it because all the other cars were new and modern, but this car was a long one; a brown estate; and unlike the other cars, older. It pulled to the front pump on the left side.

My mind was focused on getting all the cars filled as quickly as possible. I made my way around to the driver's window to ask how much she wanted me to put in. I noticed that the car, despite its age, looked to be in perfect condition. The paintwork was like new. The window opened slowly but not fully, and I heard a very soft voice: "Can you put twenty dollars in please?" She had a glow about her.

I walked around to open the cap to put the pump in. A warm feeling started to come over me, but in the busyness of the station, I didn't have time to think about it fully. I went to tend to the other cars, some of which were getting full tanks and would take longer to fill compared to just twenty dollars' worth.

As I stood waiting on the cars to get filled up, all of a sudden they were all done, and it was just me and the brown estate at the front pump. There was a silence; it was weird. I took the pump out of the car, locked the cap, and started to make my way back around to the window. I tapped the window and waited for it to come down. The lady looked old yet had a young face, without a line or a wrinkle. She was so vibrant that there was light beaming from her. She was glowing. Her hair was white, a picture of pure perfection.

I asked her for the money for the fuel, and as I reached into the car, she took me by the wrist. I panicked a little and started to pull back, but at the same time, she held on firmer. An overwhelming sense of peace came over me. I can't explain the connection I was feeling. My whole body felt like it was plugged into the universe. It was amazing.

I was talking to myself in my head: *What is happening? I really feel like crying, but I feel so safe, so connected to this lady. Am I in the twilight zone?* I stopped trying to pull back, and then she spoke to me again in the softest voice ever. I looked into her eyes. They were like no other eyes I had ever seen—they were full of love, light, and purity. She looked right into my soul. Her light reminded me of things I had seen before in the past and as a child. She glowed and emanated beautiful light.

"Robert, don't worry. You are safe," she said.

How does she know my name?

"I came here today to see you," she continued.

"What do you mean?" I asked.

She let go of my wrist. "Your call has been answered."

The look on my face must have been priceless. I was shocked and stunned. This surreal experience was happening with no shadows, voices, or flashes, just this beautiful light coming from this lady.

"You have been asking for a sign."

I nodded yes. *Oh, my God!* I was hopping out of my skin!

"I came here today to bring you your sign." She reached over, picked up a piece of cloth, turned to me, and opened it. She took out a coin that had a cross cut from its center and placed it in my hand. "Here is your sign. This coin comes to you as a message from heaven. This coin represents your strength and faith—all the things that you are. I came today to help you, to bring you the message of hope. This coin has come to you so you can help many other people."

All I could do was blink.

"I am your guardian angel, Robert, sent by God. I have manifested in this way because if it was any other shape or form, you would not have been able to understand. The easiest way for you to understand me is in the physical. God has been with you since the beginning of time, always by your side, and I came today to show you your true path and to tell you he is real."

I was in shock—I could hardly believe that this was real. I had been screaming with every thought in my mind, body, and soul for a sign, and now my guardian angel was physically with me. This was real. *Oh, my God!*

"God has made this happen. It's time to put your faith back in God and his angels. God's love for you will never change no matter how angry you think you are. God will never deny you. Your anger has brought you to a place of feeling lost and hurt. Your anger attracts the darkness that you are, but you are also light. There have been many bridges to cross in your lifetime. What I have to tell you, so you can tell others, is that he has never abandoned you, nor has he ever abandoned anyone else. He is always there with you all from the highest high to the lowest low, helping and guiding. This is the way it has been and always will be."

I literally could not believe what I was hearing.

"We are the silent workers. It's not our job to be visible to all at every moment, even though we are always helping. God has chosen for you to live on this earth so you can experience this life through the physical, mental and the emotional bodies, thus helping you to learn the lessons of the soul; the lessons of love and compassion; the lessons of kindness and forgiveness, giving and receiving. We are here to guide you, but I am your guardian angel. I have a very different job than other angels. I act like a filter, keeping you safe along your journey and only intervening with God's will as part of your soul's agreement."

"Like a filter to my life?" I asked.

"Yes. You have been mostly asleep in this one, and up until this point, it has been your soul's agreement. This was so you could work through your karma. God will help you to remember everything, but that will come in time. You will receive all the answers you seek, and you will be able to bring wisdom from other lifetimes to this one, helping you and others."

"Will I really?"

"Yes. God will be with you even more now, along with his angels—just like it is for all the other souls on this earth.

"God has no favorites," she continued. "God's love is equal in heaven and on earth. God's love is vast and goes beyond your thinking. It's time for you to understand that there is no greater gift than the gift of life. The answer you are seeking here is service and how best to serve others. This is the only path. Your understanding will come when you find yourself again and open the wisdom of your heart. Meditation will be the path to attainment."

"Okay," I said plainly, because at this point, I had little understanding of the wisdom of my heart. My mind had not yet recapitulated.

"We are unconditional love, and even that is an understatement. There are no real words that can describe us angelic beings. We come from a place on high. I came to tell you to look deep into your heart and soul, for it is there you will find the answer. You already know it's time to awaken, and you will help souls on this earth to do the same. This is part of your path. You will remember who and where you come from, and then you will help others to remember, too."

I was stunned. All this had happened as I stood in the forecourt of the garage. My guardian angel had just manifested to me. Yeah, crazy—I know. I knew I was part of it, yet I felt like I was not.

I was listening intently to every word she said, feeling massive waves of love and healing. It was like I was a computer that had crashed but had just gotten a reboot and was getting new software. I was obtaining the blueprints for this lifetime. Her beautiful glow was indescribable. She looked like complete and utter perfection.

"You have had the choice to make your own decisions from the moment you came onto this earth. But it was your soul's agreement to meet me today."

"What do you mean?" I asked.

"It's time to listen, dear one. You have many gifts that you brought here; you can use them for good or evil. This will be your choice, and it can lead you either to darkness or great light. But regardless of this, God will never leave your side."

I looked at her directly. "I don't want to be dark. I want to be free of all the things that weigh me down, all the hurts and pains."

"These things are all part of your experience, and you choose how you face them. You can either face them with love or hate, but there will never be a time of not facing them. You all have to see your shadows. Freedom of choice is the world's biggest gift. Accepting responsibility is what you have to do. This will help to set you free."

"Responsibility?"

"Yes, responsibility: for every single thought, action, feeling, and emotion, happy or sad. These are your own thoughts and have never been our thoughts or the making of heaven. They have been the making of man and woman. By taking responsibility for these things, you take responsibility for your own creations, not the creations of others."

I listened intently.

"I came to help awaken you. You are a very powerful healer. You won't understand this for some time, though. The feelings and visions that you have been experiencing all your life are very real.

"I am the validation sent to you from God. You have been seeing and sensing things around you from way back when you were a child. That was us, but you were also sensing a lot of darkness—you had to see both sides to fulfill this lifetime's journey."

I blinked a few times. "The darkness?"

"Yes. From a child, you could see the darkness around people. You were so sensitive. This is why you had so much anger and could not control it, but you also saw the light, and since a young age, you have been helping souls. Your mother will be part of the answer to this. You will have to speak to her, as your mother holds the key to the parts of your life you don't understand. She also needs healing.

"Through your mother, you will understand your past and why things were the way they were so that you can unlock some of your childhood memories."

My mind was racing. "What happened to me? I can't remember much of my childhood, but when I do, it's like I have this energy going through me. It's like a million volts that I cannot control."

"Yes, the knowledge for this will come, but not today, dear one. God has been watching over you and guiding you to this day. I will help you to understand all that is you. You will help people to learn how to heal themselves, guiding them to see the light that is within. You will help others to understand the path of karma through unconditional love and forgiveness."

"But I've had a mental blockage. I don't know how."

"You will have to work on yourself as a person, as it will not all come easy. Learn to harness things first, and then there will come a time when they will be in your memory as if they had never left you. This is when you'll be ready to help others to remember theirs. Every soul can choose to connect to God. There is no separation.

"You all have your own unique way to connect, and no man or woman has a greater gift than the other. You are all gifted."

This was what I had needed to hear. Deep down, I had always known that this was the case, but it was this confirmation that really set me free. I knew right then that I was heading in the right direction.

"From this day on, your connection is sealed. I am with you at every moment, to help you, protect you, and there will be many more to help you along the way. Not every angel will come from the other side. You will meet people on your journey in the physical that will also help you. They are called earth angels. This will help you fine-tune your own ability to understand and discern."

"How can I do this?" I asked.

"Do not worry. We will send the right people, but in divine timing. It's like learning to walk before you can run—the art of meditation. This will take so much discipline and won't be easy, as you choose to work through life's lessons. Do not give up. It will become easier as time goes."

"So you're saying I have to be patient?"

"Precisely." She smiled. "Remember: be humble and focus on service and how you can best serve others. I have told you that God has not one favorite, nor does God give to someone more than the other. Be humble for the life you live, and your life will be abundant. It's not about shouting out and naming your gifts; it's about living in them. It's about acknowledging the truth of them and walking in honest shoes. You will also have to learn this lesson again, but don't give up. The answers will come as you need them. Knock and the door will open; seek and you shall find."

"But how can I do all of this? I will never be able to do all this."

"Faith, dear one. The road is your journey. Have patience as I tell you. He was with you every step of the way, from birth to this very point. He has been with you at every experience. I know you want all the answers. The answers for you are not quite ready to come, but they will in time. As I said, speaking to your mother will help you to unlock so much. You must learn patience. You can't have everything now or your life would have no meaning.

"Your life will unfold like the lotus flower, revealing something new all the time. Have patience—all good things come to those who wait."

I began shuffling on the spot. This was surreal.

"He was with you on New Year's Eve in your apartment. He saw your pain as you looked into the mirror. You felt so lost and alone. You had a flashback. He took you out of your body and back to the nightclub when you were high on drugs, to the night you fell and banged your head. He took you back so you could see your light, so you could see his presence as he watched over you."

"I don't know who I was back then," I replied. "After I banged my head that night, I saw you all around the people in the club. I knew it was real, but I was in so much darkness that I suppressed this."

"We know. You were taken back to that point so you could see that we were always there with you. You were taken back so you could look and learn," she confirmed.

"When I stood crying in the mirror that night, I know I was taken back to see you by my side and see all the other angels around people. I closed back down after I came back to my apartment. Why have I had so much fear about you? I don't understand."

"All you hold is locked deep within your mind. It will take time for you to understand. We promise you will receive every answer. Some may be very hard to understand, and some won't. As I have already told you, take responsibility—it's part of your growth. Love is and always will be the only one true answer. To thyself always be true."

"Who writes the rules I am living in?" I asked.

"You do! The choices you make can take you on many journeys; it's time to start living by this. If you can think it, dream it, feel it, and see it, then you can be it! You are the creator of your own thoughts. You can live in darkness or in light, as you have chosen in your past. It's your past that will shape your present. This has enabled you to learn who you are again. This is all part of your plan."

"*My* plan?"

"Your plan or path is unique. It hasn't been God's will, or our will, that has chosen your lifetime or lessons, it has been thy will—the journey of the soul. Do you understand?"

"So ... I am choosing everything?"

"Yes, so be careful about what you wish or what you wish upon others. Live by the ones who have come before you—Jesus Christ, Buddha, Krishna—and their great teachings. Be kind, be loving, be humble, be compassionate. Respect yourself and others, and they will respect you. Forgive, and you will be forgiven. Hate, and hate will be you. An act of kindness will far exceed any other act when coming from a place of love. Give but not to receive. When you give not to receive, this is when you will most receive. These are only simple teachings, but they have the most meaning. People have forgotten to live this way. That is why there is such disharmony on this earth. Do you remember the train ride when you were arrested?"

"Yes," I quietly replied.

"Before you went down the flight of stairs at the train station, the words *slow down* came into your mind. That was him, helping you, guiding you, but you were not open and did not know how to trust. God has been trying to help you find a place of trust—it has taken many knocks and bangs for you. It was not your time to leave America because there was so much more for you to come through. We were just trying to help you listen. When the police officer arrested you, you were surrounded with the light of the Holy Spirit. This kept you safe. We also brought other help into your life."

Oh, my God. I thought of my friend, John, the police officer who had given me the PBA card in case I ever got stopped. "Did you help with this too?"

"Yes, that was us."

"I heard you that day, but I thought it was my mind talking, just like other times."

"We know. You have been a hard one to awaken. God can and does communicate to the mind through thought form; it's just that people don't listen. When they do, they don't trust because they are becoming so desensitized. God is communicating with everyone; some souls have just become a little bit more aware and in tune. There have been many helpers that have come to you throughout your life so far."

"Have you been with me during other times?"

"I have to tell you that the night of the accident, Independence Day, when you were down by the beach, you had many angels with you, helping you with all the other people. There was much light there. He was with you that night as you lay pinned to the floor. You have been feeling his presence from a child, but on that night, he really allowed you to feel the energy. I am your assigned messenger, a job given to me by God. It will always be our job to watch over you, dear one. So when you lay there, you came out of your body. You were watched over because this was not your time."

As she told me this, it was like I had just remembered that part of the accident. When I heard the bang, I was out. The first thing in my memory was my grandfather, which gave me a feeling of being safe or protected.

"Yes, that was him helping you also. He will help you so much from now on."

This really touched my heart. "My grandfather was really there?"

"Yes, Paddy, your grandfather. So the reason for this accident was to finally push you to a place where you would begin to let go of your demons that have lingered around you since you were a child. It is never God's aim to hurt anyone, but the soul's journey is to let go and find oneness so that we can stand in unity with God, the great *I Am* presence. You have also come into this world to release demons and to heal the wounds of your past lifetimes. What you couldn't see at this time was your light and how much you were loved, so you subconsciously started to revert to your darkness."

This really hit me. The darkness was something I feared. I didn't want to go back there.

"This is when the dark soul of the night would start to impress on you. We were sending and showering you in much light, but you could not see—the veil was truly covering you. So as you spent the next few weeks slipping away, it was your ego mind that had given up and was very much controlling how you moved forward. How you choose is always there, and we cannot and will not intervene outside of God's universal laws. That's how it's written. Your light started to diminish, and as it did, you started to disconnect from your higher self. He never left you. Do you understand?"

"I know now," I said.

She kept reinforcing that he was with me. That felt so comforting. It really put me into a place of ease like never before.

This is totally amazing. I am having a conversation with my guardian angel. Quick, pinch yourself! Your life has meaning!

"Dear one, there has always been love around you, but you had chosen to go to the depths of your darkness to find your light. How far you would go was up to you and the choices you made in this life."

"So only through my darkness could I find my light?"

"Yes, this is true: from darkness to light."

My guardian angel surrounded me in pure, unconditional love at every moment of this conversation. I had a life for which I should be so grateful, yet I had lost all sight of what was important. I was remarkably grateful in this moment. *Thank you, God.*

After these moments of revelation, we spoke about my trying to kill myself.

"He was with you more in your time of need than ever before. You needed him because you had chosen your darkness—the dark soul of the night was upon you."

I could feel my eyes welling up, thinking of that night as she spoke. "The universe will always give you what you focus on most. When your sister left for home, you had chosen to stay and end your life, and he was still by your side."

"All I could see was the darkness. I couldn't see the light, and as the dark soul of the night called, I saw it. I felt like it took me piece by piece. I was listening," I replied.

"Yes, it was at this time that your light was so diminished that you had only one particle of light within. The rest was darkness. He never stopped shining light on you."

"I didn't know how to handle my emotions. I just wanted to die. I felt I had nothing to live for. I felt I had no meaning," I cried.

"It's okay. Don't worry—we come not to judge. There is no measure for the greatness from which you and I come. God does not condemn you. God loves you—every atom and molecule is his greatest creation. You will help others to heal and find the power within them. God has a plan for every single soul that walks this earth. God has not created your pain, because this will be the will of man. God has given you the tools you need to fulfill your destiny. Learning to use the tools in a place of love, not the ego where love cannot exist, will be your challenge."

The tears were really falling now.

"Dear one, on the night you tried to take your life, your soul cried out to the heavens. The demon had its grip on you, and it was then that God intervened. Because your soul cried from such depths of despair for forgiveness and love, God's light moved in to save your soul."

I said, "I remember crying, feeling angry and hurt. I took the tablets and drank the liquor. I felt like a lost soul, and nothing else existed. I remember looking at my mother's painting of Jesus Christ's hands and thinking, *What have I done?* I was screaming out, 'Please save me. Please forgive me, for I know not what I do.' The next thing I knew, I woke up with the phone in my hand."

"Yes, that was he. He intervened divinely and Jesus Christ helped save you. It was the only way it could happen. It was he who got the phone and phoned your uncle. It was he who kept you safe from your darkness. That was the last time you will ever be in that place. You have released the karma to the light, for a place of love. It is love that will conquer all."

"My room was so bright. That was God?"

"Yes, the light was the Father, his son Jesus Christ, the Holy Spirit."

"What am I?" I asked.

"You are that which comes from the most perfect thing you will ever know, and the love from this is endless. You are an infinite being, just like your creator: never ending. You are all that there is."

There was so much information to take in. *How will I remember everything?* I reminded myself that I was on the garage forecourt. Time stood still. As my mind started to wonder, she said, "Don't worry, dear one, you will remember."

I was amazed at every moment. I felt so alive, thinking, *My life is not going to be the same after this. I want to be free.*

"In time, you will be free. You will grow and your wisdom will grow to set you and others free. Remember when you were really thinking about your mother? It was he that played her song on the radio to let you know the love she has for you."

"What? You can play songs on the radio?"

"Yes, that is one of the many things that can happen. We have been sending signs to you throughout your life, just like we have for all the other souls on this earth. The time is coming when people will understand and wake up. But you must pay attention and watch for the signs, as they are not always in the big picture.

"They can be as subtle as the smell of a flower or the sound of a song. There will always be signs."

The signs were a positive thing for me, and I enjoyed hearing about them. I vowed at that moment to keep my eyes peeled for many more.

"There is no separation," she continued. "Every single thing is connected. There are many angels walking and working on this earth at this moment, and there will be more to come as things change. Your mother is going through a lot of pain; like many other souls on this planet, she carries lots of hurt. There will be many lessons you will learn from your mother: forgiveness and unconditional love. Your mother, deep down, loves you dearly, and you will both, one day, find balance. You will see each other's light. Don't worry, she will be fine."

I felt so emotional at this moment.

"You will still doubt life, even after I leave today. It's nearly my time to go."

"I won't. I promise I won't."

She smiled. "It's okay. You have your faith back now, and that will never leave you again. You have your coin, and this is part of your soul's awakening. There will be people who will come into your life, and your spiritual journey, who will try and hurt you. They will not understand you, and they will try to destroy your good name.

"Remember, it is your light that they see, not your darkness. It's your light they will most fear."

"What do you mean by this? Please tell me."

She never answered. She just smiled in the most loving way.

I wasn't ready to hear the answer. Or maybe I had to go through the experience to really understand it. Time would tell.

"There will be some challenges you have to face, dear one. There will be some major lessons. You really need to listen now. Remember who you really are, not what they want you to become. You will face the darkness of the soul of the night once more, but not like before. This time, you will know thyself. You will tread in your old shoes again and be on and off your path. But don't fear, for we will never leave you."

No," I pleaded. "I don't want to go there again."

"It won't be the same. Forgiveness will be the only answer—hold no judgment. This is what will finally bring you to your soul. The Light of God is within each and every soul on this planet. Deep within, you've asked the same question all your life."

"How come I have been searching for my teacher all my life, knowing that he is here? From a child, when I would go to a church or hear a story, deep within me, I'd always known that he would be here and never leave here. He lives continually, just like each and every one of us. And why is reincarnation not spoken about? Why is this not a primary part of our beliefs?"

"By 2009, this one question that you're asking will be answered, and you will never look back. This will be the beginning of a whole new time. Remember to write— keep a dairy at all times. This is very important."

"Yes, okay. I will."

"There will come a time when they will become your books. They will be your salvation, but also the guide for your books. Use your writing as an outlet, to connect to your higher self."

"So I am writing books?" I questioned.

"Yes, dear one, you will tell your story, bringing new and relative information to others. It's important that the message is clear and to share the message of hope. This world is coming into a place where there will be great changes. The world needs hope, the light of God and the love of God. This is universal. It comes from a place of no attachment. God is real, you are real, and I am the validation of this. Remember, focus on being the healer and on your intuitive connection to the light, but you will walk in the lower vibration, which we call lower psychic nature. From this, there will be many tough lessons. Focus on God no matter what."

God had always been my focus; I just didn't know it till then. "Thank you so much," I said.

"It's my time to go now. God will always be with you, guiding you along your path. Your coin will stay with you, until one day, it is your turn to come back. Keep it safe as it is a special gift from heaven. It will help bring healing to many. Remember, healing is your biggest gift."

"Will I ever see you again?" I asked. "Where do you live?" My rational and logical mind started to kick in. *After meeting my guardian angel, who brought me a gift and helped me understand all the things I am, my connection to God, and how we all share the same thing, I ask her if she lives close to me. How silly am I?* I had just received all the proof and validation I had asked for, yet I couldn't help but doubt what had just happened.

Before I could question her further, she pulled out of the garage and was gone.

I was buzzing. I danced and jumped around the forecourt of the garage. What a surreal, energetic moment. I had been asking—quite literally *praying*—for this moment, but still, I was never prepared for how great it would feel.

God, you have answered my call, and this is not the first time. Thank you so much, God. I love you. This world is real, and there is life after death. I have a purpose, a meaning. What a day! I can't wait to go home and tell Brian and Tammy!

I waited for my shift to end, which felt like an eternity! All I could think about was what had just happened. I had dreamt many things in my life, but this was very surreal. I spent the rest of that working day holding my coin. It was electric! I was buzzing with excitement for my life.

A little while later, I ran home. I burst through the door like a madman, ranting about how I had just met my guardian angel. Brian and Tammy looked at me like I was crazy! I was the one who had been asking God for the sign, not them, so they were fairly confused. I can totally understand why; I wasn't explaining it too well with all my excitement.

I went to my room and spent a few hours in silence. I started doubting then, listening to my ego and asking if it was real. This miracle had just happened to me, but I started to question it and all my fears and insecurities came up. *What if they don't believe me?* My room was the stillest it had ever been, with no flashes, shadows, or lights.

I went back upstairs that evening for dinner and spoke to Brian and Tammy. I explained what I had experienced that day, and as I started to talk in more detail, they were in as much shock as I was. For some strange reason, my ego mind was working hard on me.

I spoke to Brian about this as I felt it was coming from a place of doubt. explained *ego* and its meaning. He told me that it was an acronym:

$$E = Ease, \ G = God, \ O = Out.$$

I would have to learn to still my mind and thoughts. Brian pushed me more toward beginning to practice meditation; he said that would be a good foundation. Up until this point I had never put my focus into really practicing meditation, so this, in a way, was new to me. I was only at the start of this new part of my journey, of my awakening. I placed my coin on my bedside altar, which now became my angel altar, this felt so special. Brian told me to take the time to connect to myself; he thought this would help me a lot. I was also reading a new book that reinforced what he was telling me.

Before I met my guardian angel, I had all these strange experiences when I went to bed at night, and now there was complete silence. I was trying to understand everything my guardian angel had told me. I continued the conversation in my mind, but still there was silence—no shadows, lights, or anything being moved around my room.

I started to write. I went to bed at the same time every evening to begin my ritual. I lit a candle and breathed deeply to relax my body and mind. I placed my hands on my body—the heat this generated was extraordinary, like an oven! I remembered the heat from the neighbor who had helped me before I came to America, only my hands were much hotter. It felt as if someone had lit a fire on them.

I placed my hands on different parts of my body, and the ease and relief I felt was profound. I later discovered that these were my chakras and that I was self-healing. My guardian angel had told me to focus on healing. *Is this what she meant?*

I was in a routine. I think I was trying to force it, but the silence still continued. The doubting Thomas within was working hard. I was back in my rational mind.

Every day at work, I asked the locals if they had ever seen the car that my guardian angel had been driving or if they knew her. Guess what? Not one person knew her or her car. I was desperate for answers. I thought meeting her that day would change my life there and then—*presto*—everything would be in harmony.

I felt myself getting pissed off and angry. I was very frustrated. I wanted it all there and then. I hadn't truly listened to what she had told me. Patience is what she encouraged: "When the time is right he is always with you."

I tried so hard to see with my physical eyes that I was totally blocking my mind. I spent my time writing in my diary. Looking back, I can see now how the writing helped me to release my anger. The things I wrote in my first diary were incredibly dark, but as my guardian angel had told me, this would help me find myself. I was letting go, clearing the past so I could make way for the present.

I stopped asking about her at the garage. I knew in my heart that it was her, and my coin was my validation. When I held it, I could feel the energy and connection from it. I held it at night as I meditated.

Brian and I had a deep conversation. He told me he could see my gifts but that I was still blinded. He also said that one day I would work with the angels and that when I opened up, the whole universe would open up for me. I could not see this. I felt that silence was my enemy, but what I failed to see was that silence was my friend.

Brian recommended I go to see a medium he knew. I agreed but was totally skeptical. Everything at the beginning of my journey came from the left brain. I was looking for solid, concrete answers, even though I had my coin. I became very rigid in my thoughts, and this blocked my intuition.

The best advice Brian gave me was to learn how to control my gift. If I didn't, I would crash and burn. I had to be patient. I agreed with, and believed in, what he was saying. I thought it was only special people who had gifts. Even though God's message was that there is no one soul more special than another, I was conflicted at the time—all part of the process of learning.

And let me tell you, I was not special. I was as normal in my eyes as everyone else.

I went to my room that evening and let myself go. I lay in bed by the candlelight. I placed my hands on my forehead and started to breathe slowly, in through my nose and out through my mouth. I felt myself drifting into a semiconscious state, and I started to become aware of something else in my room. The feelings were back, the same as the day I had met my guardian angel. My senses heightened, and my whole body became electrified.

I removed my hands from my forehead, and my candle started to flicker. The flame grew from one inch in height to about ten. My room was bathed in light, and my body felt as if I had been plugged into the main electrical panel. I began to notice a very sharp ringing in my ears. It felt as if someone was screaming at a frequency I had never heard before. I spent most of that night going through this experience.

When I woke up the next day, I knew that things would never be the same. I spent three full days in the house, going through a massive body cleanse. I must have visited the bathroom over a hundred times in three days! It was as if my body had just experienced a massive shock. My bedroom became my training ground.

As I lay in bed, the light from the candle would start dancing and my room would fill with amazing colorful lights. The feeling had now elevated from plugged into the main to plugged into the national grid. It was so intense!

My senses became so clear that I started to receive information. It was like I was receiving transmissions, a recapitulation—like I was being downloaded with lost knowledge of this life. It was an amazing experience, but I wasn't going out to tell the world. Things were changing and changing fast.

Brian started talking about a book he had just read. I knew exactly what he was talking about even though I had never seen a page of the book. I had an inner knowing, just one of the many things I was experiencing.

I was seeing things clearer, like the light that was around people. I was very much in tune with people's energies; my whole body was like a modem for them. I experienced the shadows and outlines again. I then became sensitive to colors and intuitively linked them to the presence of angels. I had seen these colors before—on the night of the accident at the nightclub and also at other times in my life, especially my childhood. The shadows or silhouettes weren't just spirits; some were demons.

I shared some of my experiences with Brian and Tammy. They had read many books, so they sort of knew what was going on. The one thing that stood out to me was that I never once stopped talking to God, in my heart and mind or even out loud. If I didn't get the answer directly, I kept up the conversation. I was disciplined.

One day when I was downstairs, Tammy called me to help her with something, so I went to help her. I sensed this feeling, like an energy coming from the kids' bedroom.

Tammy didn't sense it. The next thing we knew, we heard a loud bang. We both ran into the bedroom and found that it was ice cold. We stood facing each other, and all of a sudden this spirit walked right in between us. It was about six feet tall.

Tammy's face was a picture! We both stood there. The hair on the back of my neck stood up.

Tammy said, "Did you see that?"

"Yes," I said. "It walked right between us."

Tammy couldn't believe her eyes. She asked me again if it had been real. We could see through it—its shape and full outline. It was transparent. We both couldn't wait to tell Brian. A lot of activity was going on around the house. I don't remember being afraid. I had no fear whatsoever. If anything, it was a little exciting and I wanted to experience more! But I was also mindful and wanted to be present.

I kept reading my book. It discussed spirit guides and said that these beings have a totally different job than angels. I began to ask my spirit guides to reveal themselves to me.

16

Everything Happens for a Reason

*Watch and pray that you may not enter into
temptation. (Matthew 26:41 ESV)*

I could sense many different energies and tried to figure them out. I felt differences among the varying types of energies. This may not be the same for everyone, but it was true for me.

In my bedroom, doing my usual routine of writing in my diary while asking mental questions, I asked very precise questions of my higher self, to God, his angels, and spirit guides. I sat up while writing and asked, *What's your name? I can sense you.*

The ringing in my ears became sharp, but I kept asking. I felt the warmth and the energy pull back. I got a light chill and a tingle on my face. I asked again, *What is your name? Why won't you let me hear? Please tell me your name!* Next, the sharp ringing stopped, and I heard the name Danny in my mind. It sounded like it was a mile away. I asked again, *Is your name Danny?*

This time I heard it loud and clear: "Danny is my name. I am your spirit guide."

I nearly fell out of the bed. Wow, I had made my first connection! Instead of feeling and sensing, it was like I was discovering these things from my higher self. My life was taking a turn toward the thing that was deep within me. I was living a life with purpose.

In my mind, I asked lots of questions, especially at night. Even though I knew there were many different ways to communicate, I knew it would be easier to communicate through my mind and my thoughts. This was one big learning process. This would help me understand.

Through my thoughts, I asked why I had so much heat in my hands. "This heat is the energy of the universe," Danny answered. "It comes from God. It is given freely to each and every living being on this earth. You will use this energy to help others heal."

"Are you with me at every moment?" I asked.

"No, I only come when it is my time to work with you, or if you need my guidance."

I couldn't feel any other energy around me at that moment, so I asked Danny if any other guides with me.

"Not at this time, but there will be ones that will come and go for different life lessons, just like I will go when it's my time."

"Will you not be my guide forever?" I asked.

"No. It's up to you to learn and grow. I will be like a teacher, but I am not the one. He will come soon, and as you grow, the information that matches the vibration for that growth will come. I too have to grow; I am also on a journey."

I thanked Danny for communicating with me, but I could not see him at the time. I asked about my grandfather, Paddy.

"Very soon," he confirmed.

I cannot stress this enough: the most important thing to me here was my connection to God. When I thought of God, I imagined the sun and how bright it is, and then I thought of a light a million times stronger. This definitely worked. It also gave me a great sense of safety and security. I was aware at this time that I needed to only call from this place. I did not want to call upon lower-vibration energies that had been with me in the past.

Things were shifting for me on a spiritual level, but on a human level, I still had some obstacles. I hadn't spoken to Kim or my mother. The time was coming to face this. I felt I was stronger and starting to understand the madness that I thought I was going through. I wasn't crazy. Everything happens for a reason. I knew this now. My battle with others' thinking I was crazy was still to come.

At this point, writing was a great outlet and helped me realize many different things. As I wrote about my feelings, they sounded harsh at first, then they started to lighten up and later turned into forgiveness. I found great relief in this, and it definitely helped to ground my energy.

A Quote from One of My First Diaries

What is your pain? Pain, is it possible to turn it around? It will get hard if you fight with it, you will be surrounded with it. God, I surrender.

I surrender. I surrender to my pain and I invoke myself in love. In love. In love to you, God; for you, God; with you, God. Please let my pain be your love and turn into your love.

I finished by thanking God and my praise was with him. I used my writing as a form of venting, and it brought me to a whole new level of understanding, as well as taught me many things. When I wrote, I felt that the light of God and the Holy Spirit would always surround me.

I was learning to trust in what I was experiencing, although at times I was still a bit skeptical about the world and other things, so when Brian again mentioned going to see the medium, I finally agreed.

Somewhere in my mind, I thought, *What could he tell me?* I didn't have much faith in others. I was very cautious. This was okay, I told myself. I had just been through a major, life-changing experience and was only starting to learn to love myself. I had many barriers and didn't want to be hurt, so I kept the barriers and safety net up. Brian told me that the medium ran a meeting circle, so we would find out when the next one was and go. I became excited as I thought about going.

One morning, I was lying in bed when I felt a shift of energy in the room. It was 6:33 a.m. I started to wake up. I could feel the difference in the room temperature. I thought, *This is weird* because I usually felt warmth. I started asking questions in my mind: *How come this feels different?*

The answer came to my mind: "The warmth is not in the room. To feel within is more important than to sense outside, so look deep within and you will know us there."

I took a breath and, as right as rain, I could feel the difference. *But I can feel you in the room.*

"Yes, you can."

This conversation was held through my thoughts and targeted my heart and all my emotions.

"When your guides come to you, you will not always feel them externally, so start to become aware of what's happening inside. But always remember to put God first in everything. It's so important to remember that even though there are many realms and layers, not all of these are overshadowed by the light. We also need a filter to protect us from parts of the spirit realms or the astroplane."

"But how will I find my filter?"

"Meditation will free you from the darkness, but just like the law of attraction, what we put out there will return. God can protect you; ask him always for his light the holy spirit to watch over you. This is why it's important to always come from a place of love and light and to be aware of the anger and hatred that you can carry within your heart and mind. Do not get into the battle with your ego. It has been said before that there is no one more gifted than another, and when you bring this message to the people, there will be some who will understand. On the other hand, though, there will be some that will come from a place of ego, cannot yet understand, and are very much living in their ego and their lower-psychic nature. They have not yet realized that everything, and every aspect of them, was and is created by the divine God."

Have you ever had the experience of thinking of someone calling you, and then the phone rings and it's the person you were thinking of?

Later on that evening, Brian, Tammy, and the kids got ready to go out. They asked if I would like to come with them, but I wasn't really in the mood. I just wanted to chill, so they headed off without me.

I had been thinking about Kim all day. I was lying stretched out on the living room chair, daydreaming. About a minute after I started to think about Kim again, the phone started ringing. When I answered it, I realized it was her! My heart was in my throat, I was shaking, and she was crying. Understandably, she was very angry with me.

I tried to explain that my head had been in such a bad place that I had lost all my identity. I didn't tell her that I had tried to end my life. She wanted to know why I had left. I said that I couldn't cope after the accident and that, when my sister left, it got worse, so I came up here.

"But why haven't you answered the phone?"

I didn't have an answer for her. "I am so sorry, Kim. I really am." I started to cry. I knew I had hurt her so much after all the kindness she had shown me. I was going through this whole experience—my world had been turned upside down and inside out.

"We have both come through a really traumatic experience. The person I was before the accident was lost, and I was searching for myself. After the accident, I was in a real dark place but couldn't find it within me to tell you, and when I came to Brian and Tammy's, so many things changed for me internally. I was having a meltdown, and I began to try finding myself through God and spirituality." I tried to explain.

Kim thought I had been brainwashed and was living in a cult.

I couldn't articulate what I meant, only that I was sorry. She said that she had been going out of her mind and wondered how I could be so insensitive. This I totally understood, but I felt so trapped within myself. I was caught up in this bubble at my aunt and uncle's.

I told Kim that it was never my intention to hurt her. We didn't speak for much longer. The conversation ended very sharply, and she hung up on me without saying goodbye.

I felt immense guilt. *What have I done?*

> *When thinking about life, no amount of guilt*
> *can solve the past, and no amount of anxiety*
> *can change the future.* —Dani Johnson

I went into the living room. I was crying, surrounded by all this pain, and I was the creator of it. As I lay down on the chair, I said to myself, *I deserve this.* I was thinking about Kim, asking God for help yet again and asking the angels to go to Kim at this time, as I did not need them. I put my hands on my heart. It was like I was asking everyone for their help. I felt really tired all of a sudden. In my mind, I was asking Danny for some help.

I asked him to let me see him. *Please, Danny, I really need you.*

I drifted off to sleep. I am not sure for how long, but when I started to wake up I could feel some energy at my feet. You know when you're half awake, your eyes are trying to focus, and it's like coming from a dark room into light? That's the way it was for me.

I opened my eyes fully and there he was—Danny, standing in front of me. Danny was really tall, about six feet, two inches. He was wearing a checked red and black shirt.

I got a little fright as you would expect! I jumped and closed my eyes, and when I opened them again, he wasn't there. I started asking questions in my mind. *Where did you go?*

He told me he had been by my side for the phone call. His message was that *everything happens for a reason.* "Don't beat yourself up. We are all on a journey. You were ready to see me. I manifested to validate that everything is happening perfectly. You will get the opportunity to make peace with Kim, but she needs time to be angry and heal. When you asked the angels to help, they heard that—they have surrounded Kim with love and light."

I saw the headlights of my uncle and aunt's car as they pulled in, and with that, my communication ended. The kids were hyper. I was my usual playful self, and the kids got even more hyper.

Tammy asked if I was okay. "You look like you have been crying."

"I am fine," I lied.

I waited until later that evening, when everyone had gone to bed except Brian and me, to tell him that I had spoken with Kim, that it wasn't a nice conversation, but I did feel better. I didn't say how the phone call had happened or about Danny manifesting to me. My uncle, being the wise old soul, always seemed to have the right answers and could put things into perspective all the time—even in the worst situation he always saw the light. This was a great quality of his, and one he was teaching me. I was so grateful.

I prayed to God that night, asking and hoping that all would be okay. I asked God to never leave me and said that I wanted to live to the best of my ability.

I had some vivid dreams. A lot of the time I would come out of my body and fly to places in my dream state. I was going to "spiritual school" in a dream state. I would wake up the next day with new knowledge or a shift in my consciousness. My understanding was opening up to love, compassion, and forgiveness. I was slowly learning to forgive myself. I could now see how badly I had treated my own thoughts and feelings.

I dreamed that I saw my grandfather. He was showing me how happy he was and all the good work he was doing. Then he took me to my mother and father, showing me the love they had for me and the love I had for them. The message he brought to me was, "It's easier in life to point the finger than to accept the change. Everything will change when you change. This is the only answer."

He also showed me that night some photos that were taken at Niagara Falls and some from my apartment when

I first arrived in America. In the dream, I understood that I had something to see in them.

When I woke the next morning, I searched for the pictures, pulling my room apart. When I finally found them, I noticed that a few pictures had some smoky patterns. I looked at them all day. I knew that this was what my dream had pointed me to and wanted me to see. Angel energy was also present in the photos, as were orbs. Yet again, this was another validation that I was on the right path. I felt that this was part of my journey: to learn to trust that the light had always been around me.

I took the photos up to ask Brian and Tammy to take a look. Their thoughts were the same as mine. I had looked at these pictures loads of times before, but I had never seen these signs until now.

How come I can see them now? I asked myself. *God's light is here for all to see, but most people's vibration is not tuned into that. You went through your clearing for things to become clearer.*

It made sense to me, God is definitely over shadowing so much. The will of God moves the world.

What was even more crazy was that some of the photos had been taken when I first arrived in America on a disposable camera. Many people said things like energies and orbs like these could only be captured on a digital camera, but I was being given evidence at every opportunity.

It was time for me to put my faith into action, get out of the left brain, and stop looking for logical answers all of the time. It was time for me to explore the creative side of the brain, the side with no limitations. I was being given hard evidence and proof of my life. What was shining through for me was that I was part of a bigger picture, a plan. Brian, Tammy, and I were planning to go to the medium's home that Sunday, so I decided I would take the photos to see what he could tell me.

Circle? What Is That?

On Sunday morning, I got up bright and early, feeling very excited about going to this spiritual circle. I asked Brian to explain to me exactly what a circle was. I thought everyone went there and sat around in a circle. He laughed and said, "Kind of, but at this meeting we will be sitting in rows."

I asked him what I should expect. "Who will be there?" I asked.

"All kinds of people. There will be healers, people who work with crystals, and people who work with angels," he replied.

I laughed, thinking, *Oh, my God, I am going to some hippie commune!*

I put my coin into a special little holder and packed my photos. The whole way there, all I thought about was my grandfather. I wondered if I would receive a message. I knew Brian wanted a message, to make contact, so I hoped my granddad would come to him.

The medium lived about twenty minutes away. My hands were a little sweaty and my heartbeat was a little faster than normal on the way. I asked Brian and Tammy how long it would go on for, and they said it would be a couple of hours. This was all very exciting, but as we pulled up at the house, something came over me. I became the biggest skeptic ever! I didn't say this to my uncle or aunt, though.

As we pulled into the drive, we saw lots of people standing outside the medium's house. I think I was the youngest one there! Tammy and Brian started chatting to some people outside as I checked the place out. I started chatting to a few people, who had nothing but good things to say. I was curious to see what everyone else was going on about. I stood on a side porch waiting to go in. Tammy and Brian instructed me to take off my shoes. I was thinking there would be a smell of feet inside!

Why do we have to take off our shoes? Do I have any holes in the toes of my socks?

Being a little skeptical of this guy, I figured that he had listening devices outside and inside the room so that he could listen to what people said before the group started and then come in and make a connection. I decided to sit at the very back of the room, while Brian and Tammy sat at the front. I had my arms crossed. I was guarding myself, scanning the room to see if he had planted stuff to hear what was going on.

Well, let me tell you—I was in for a shock. It was another part of the puzzle.

The circle was about to start. Silence fell over the room, and in came the medium. He wasn't what I had imagined. He introduced himself and gave us an introduction to what was going to be covered in the class. I listened, trying to fight my skepticism. He asked us to pack away the chairs and lie on the floor. Some people sat in the window seats as there wasn't enough room on the floor for everyone. His space was lovely—all wooden, white, and cream. He also had lots of crystals that I had never seen before, some of which were really big. They were beautiful.

He instructed us to lie on the floor and to get a blanket if we needed one. I wasn't sensing anything in the room. He asked us to close our eyes and focus on our breathing, which I was already doing. Then he asked us to imagine a golden white light around us and started taking us through a guided meditation, my first one. I was struggling; I found it hard for my mind to relax.

I moved around on the floor, my legs twitching. *This is a load of crap,* I thought. Everyone else seemed to just get right into it, but there was the Irish boy, moving around the floor like Michael Flatley in *Lord of the Dance*! The medium kept talking away, bringing us down a flight of stairs and counting the steps. I couldn't see them let alone count them. Then I felt hands on my head and heard his voice next to me. He had put his hands on my head. I felt pressure and heat, just like the heat I felt when I laid my hands on my body.

I felt myself getting very relaxed, going deeper and deeper. My mind wasn't racing. All the thoughts slipped away. I got to the bottom of the stairs and saw a massive symbol of two snakes intertwined, going up a sword. I could still feel hands on my head, only now I could hear the medium's voice at the other side of the room. *Who has their hands on my head?* He brought us back up the stairs and back into the room.

The second I opened my eyes I looked around the room—nobody had their hands on my head. I looked at him. People were asking lots of questions, but. I probably had a stunned look on my face.

"What did you see?" he asked me.

"I saw these two snakes that looked like they were attached to a sword with wings. I have never seen this before," I said.

"This is very powerful," he replied. "It is a symbol for kundalini, which is the movement of energy. It is part of your healing, and it highlights hope, courage, fear and surrender." He turned away and started answering other questions.

I thought, *Fear is something I have lots of, hope was my message from my guardian angel, and healing is what my angel said I did—a healer.* It was like another small piece to the jigsaw.

He spoke for a short while after this about things that were going on at the present time and then took a break. He asked if anyone wanted healing, but for some strange reason, a group of people had taken Brian outside the room. He was lying on the floor with big crystals all over his body and had lots of people around him. They were giving him a group healing. It looked very intense. I was deep in thought and feeling significant resistance but wanted to break free. I was around these people for a reason.

Brian was still on the floor. It looked like he was releasing a tremendous amount as people were laying their hands on him. It was quite something to look at. In the back of my mind, I thought, *What if people back home in Ireland could see me at this? What would they think? What would they say?*

When the break was over, we made our way back into the room. It was full of energy, very warm, and felt amazing. The medium came back and started talking, and people asked him more questions. He worked his way around the room. I was at the back—right at the back wall. If I were any farther away from him, I would have been in the garden! Before I knew it, he was standing right in front of me. He said, "You're not from here, are you?"

That wouldn't be hard to figure, I thought. *I am the only one in the room with a strong Irish accent! The only other Irish person is my uncle, but his accent has an American twang.*

He continued. "I mean, you're not from America." I didn't reply.

"You come from a small town. It's Drog …It's Drog … I can't say it!"

I knew why he couldn't say the name. It's a name that most people wouldn't be used to seeing or saying unless they were from Ireland. But he was right—my hometown is called Drogheda. The skepticism was still there a little but was slowly dissipating. He had my attention now.

"I have a man here, and he wants to bring you a message. I feel like he's your grandfather. Does the initial P mean anything?"

Yes, I thought.

"Hold on, his name is Paddy."

My grandfather's name—how did he know that?

"He also wants to call you this—mickser."

This could be nothing but a message from my grandfather. It was so accurate. The word *mickser* was my grandfather's special nickname for us kids. I had just received a massive healing. The man loved by us all was right there. I couldn't see my granddad, but I felt him and his energy as the space around us got colder.

"He also wants to say he has a dog here with him. The dog loves rocks or stones and hasn't a tooth in his head! Hold on—Bruce. Do you know this name?"

"Yes, that was our dog," I replied. "We grew up with him as children. He hadn't a tooth in his head!"

This held even more meaning for me. Bruce had been poisoned, and I had spent a few days trying to get him to eat and drink before he died. I felt so sad inside.

He then mentioned my mother and about our not speaking. "You need to contact her."

I nodded, knowing exactly what he meant.

"Your grandfather loves you dearly." And with that, the communication ended.

I was so happy inside. What more could I have asked for? I didn't mention my coin or took it out to show anyone. I didn't get to show him the photos, but I knew the time wasn't right.

About half an hour later, the circle was coming to an end when a woman introduced herself to me as Paula. She was a stunning woman. The energy coming from her was soft and gentle. She was lovely. "I am a healer. Why don't you and your uncle come for some healing?" she asked. I said I would love to, so we exchanged numbers and agreed to meet.

God's universe was starting to open my path, sending the people I needed to me. Is this what my guardian angel had meant? I made some other friends that day too, and I left no longer skeptical.

We left for home. I don't think my bum touched the seat the whole way home—I was so high on life! I thanked my grandfather for coming.

I thought, *Will I phone Mom when I get home?* I thought that maybe I would. There was a silence in the car. We were all deep in thought, our faces alight with the light of God within us. Life just kept on saying that it had meaning.

We returned and I phoned home. My brother Joe answered, my first challenge. It was small but still a challenge. Brian and Tammy had been chatting to people at home and must have said something like, "You won't know Robbie when you see him. He's a changed man."

Well, they took this in a different way than intended. Joe is the biggest joker ever. He started taking the piss out of me, saying, "I hear you are all holy now! You're going to mass and everything—you have been converted!"

I felt a little defensive and said to him, "You wouldn't understand."

"Sure, I would," he joked. "You are a Bible basher now."

"Do you believe in God, Joe?" I asked.

"Yeah," he replied.

"Well, why do you mock God?" There was a silence. He didn't know what to say back to that.

I loved my brother so much, but it was the only answer that came to mind. I acknowledged myself and the part of God that lives within me. I never said it to hurt him, nor did he say what he said to hurt me. But this was only the beginning of people's projection and negativity toward me.

My mom got on the phone next, and I told her that I had been to see the medium. "He told me lots of things, and I knew deep inside that we should speak. I'm sorry. I love you."

This was a very difficult time for me. There were many deep scars of hurt and pain within. And ultimately, I really just wanted my relationship with my mom to be on track and in harmony with the world.

There will be times when you will feel like you're on your knees, when all hope seems to be fading away. If you have ever gone into a room and it is in complete darkness, and you light a candle, the candle will light up the room. There will always be shadows where the light reflects off things in the room, but with the candlelight, the darkness cannot quench the light.

The darkness will never dampen out the brightness of the light.

The only way the darkness will ever go is if it turns into light. Life will bring us only what we can handle— nothing more and nothing less. Our family, friends, and relationships in this life are so complex, yet so easy. When we learn to come from a place of love, this will be when we most shine bright and our light will be like the lighthouse guiding the ships from a stormy sea.

Always remember that the light from the lighthouse will shine, but it cannot stop ships from crashing onto rocks. So, love many and forgive even more, for the eyes of hope are shining on you once more.

My Light Was Shining Bright

We all sat around the table that night, chatting about the day. My uncle was so happy for me. He could see me changing. My light was starting to shine again, and I was on cloud nine. I was happy that I had spoken to my mom. I had my faith; it was unbreakable. And for the first time in a very long time, I knew my life was real. I knew that God was real, and I had this feeling of fullness within me.

Brian and I were excited about going to see Paula for some healing. There was something more to her. She had a beautiful presence and a sense of purity. We were lucky to have met her.

I began seeing lots of number sequences at this time on clocks, the TV, and license plates—for example, 4:44, 5:55, 9:11, or 11:11. I felt drawn to numbers. Brian had a book about them, so we took it out and looked at what some of these sequences meant. It also spoke about the law of attraction. I noticed that when events were happening around me, these numbers would flash on clocks or the TV. This was all part of my spiritual growth, reminding me that the universe is always in sync.

Brian and I were messing around with a deck of cards as we spoke more about our recent experience. He said, "I told you he was good."

I asked, "Do you think this is what I will do? What do you think my journey is going to be?" Even though after seeing the medium that day I really could see what I was going to do, I still wasn't exactly sure how I was going to get there. Even though my guardian angel had told me my path, it was like I was still seeking further guidance or reassurance from Brian.

"Yes, Robbie, you will work with people and help them. You have a great journey ahead of you," he affirmed.

I told Brian that when I lay in bed at night, I received information like I was plugged into the World Wide Web. Anything I looked for in my mind would be there. I knew he understood, but sometimes when someone else is explaining their experience, it can be very hard for others to fully understand if they have not experienced the same things. I explained it the best way I could.

We set little challenges for each other each night. This evening we got a whole deck and placed the cards face down on the table. We would take turns picking a card—for example, Brian would point at a card and say, "What is that one?"

I would say, "Four of clubs," and he would turn it over. If it was the four of clubs, I would take another turn.

Brian picked, and I went first. "What's this one, Robbie?"

Out of my mouth came the words, "Six of diamonds." He turned it over, and I had gotten it right! And the next one—the two of spades, right again. Then the six of diamonds. The look on Brian's face was priceless!

How am I doing this? I thought.

We kept on going. The only way I can explain what was happening is that, when Brian would ask me to guess a card, a strong feeling would come over me, and out of my mouth came the name of the card.

That night I guessed every single card in the deck except two. I couldn't believe it. I would say my intuition at this time was most pure, as I had no other influence from the outside world. It was a straight connection back to my higher self. It was like a child who comes into the world with his or her gifts, and everything flows freely with no fear or judgment. It wasn't that I was special. This was coming from a place of complete trust, just like all the gifts that come with each and every one of us.

I was lucky to be in a place where I was surrounded by love so I was able to nurture the natural side of my ability and to connect to my higher self and God. I was so excited and grateful at this time in my life. I began to understand even more about myself, but I still needed to search my earlier life for some other answers. They were definitely making their way toward me, without my even knowing.

As I reflected on my conversation with my guardian angel, a phrase appeared in my mind once more: *There is not one soul here that is more gifted than another.* I began to understand that part of my path would be to help others make it out of the darkness and into the light and that I would do this through my own personal experiences.

This brought me back to the question, *What did she mean when she brought me the message of hope? And how does this serve others?* I was looking for the answer because this was a fragment of the key to my path in life.

I went to bed that night and asked God for the answer. *What does hope mean? Please tell me!* I started writing in my diary, but the answers still did not come. It was like the silence had arrived again, only this time, I understood it. I didn't jump into a place of fear or think the presences had left. I just accepted that they never leave us and that they cannot bring us every single answer or do this twenty-four-seven, for that is not the will of God.

We as humans have to live out our own experiences in order to learn. If I was caught up in this way of thinking all the time, I would miss out on the biggest gift I had been given—the gift of *life*! Don't we all expect answers right then and there? And when the answers don't come directly, we can easily fall out of sync. Let me tell you, I had no choice but to wait and learn that God's universe has laws, and within those laws we must abide. *Divine timing*. I needed to focus more on meditation, and I would. I was beginning to learn the art of patience.

17

Healing Hands: It's What's in Your Heart

Brian and I contacted Paula to arrange our healing. I was really looking forward to it. It was such a treat to be around like-minded people. We had booked our session for Tuesday evening. Brian explained that healers put their hands on or off your body and fill you with the light of God, coming from a place of unconditional love. This helps other people on their path to self-healing.

I was very excited. I already knew Paula had a really strong and special energy and I wondered whether I would tell Paula about my coin and my guardian angel. I wasn't sure, so I decided to just go with the flow. My thoughts were still with God, and I was still asking many questions: *Hope—what is the meaning?*

At 5:55 p.m., it was time for us to make our way to Paula's house. We arrived and rang the doorbell. As Paula answered the door, I saw massive rays of light behind her, nearly blinding me! Angels were all around her, and the energy in her home was amazing. I felt an instant connection to her. When I looked into her eyes, I felt like we had a soul connection.

She offered us some tea, and we both took an herbal tea. She then asked who wanted to go first. Brian went first for his treatment while I waited in her living room. The whole time I was there, it was full of beautiful light and energy, and this continued to shift while Brian was having his healing. It was quite a surreal experience and also very peaceful.

When Brian came out from his healing, he looked different, like he was floating and super relaxed. I was still contemplating telling her about my coin when she took me into her healing room. It was beautiful. Everything had its perfect place. She started explaining what healing was and how it would work for me. She asked if I ever had a healing before. I was just about to say no when I remembered that my neighbor had given me a massage before I left for America, but I decided not to say anything at the time. I also didn't tell her about the heat in my own hands and that when I put them on my body, I could feel massive waves of heat passing through. She explained that she would put her hands on different points of my body called chakras, each of which has a different color and meaning. I nodded. I knew about chakras, but I wasn't a master on them.

Paula had a specialized bed. I lay down, and she put a blanket over me. I closed my eyes and started to drift off. I could feel the heat from Paula's hands. Holy moly, it was like I was sitting on the beach at midday! It felt like pressure was all over me. In fact, it started to feel like my chakras were aligning. Then I experienced a massive release, and my whole body tingled. She started to speak to me.

"Robbie, you are very special. You have come here to help people. You have many angels with you. You also see angels and have since you were a child. Your vision will become clearer. You saw lots of light when you came here today. This is the light of God and his angels. These are just some of the energies you will come across through your work as you help other people along their journey.

"What I have to tell you is that you have healing hands, and when the time is right, you will use them."

I was in a place of pure bliss. I drifted further and further, deeper and deeper. I heard her voice call me, "It's time to come back into the room."

I started to wake up, or come back. I saw her standing about two feet away, yet I felt her hands on me! She smiled. "There were many angels here tonight," she shared. Now I know why Brian looked like he was floating—I was now floating too!

She warned me to me be careful, that I could come out of my body quite easily. She advised me to remember to always ground myself like the roots of a sycamore tree. I understood a bit but not fully.

We went back out into the living room, and Paula asked what I thought of the circle.

"I found it very good and helpful," I replied. In the back of my mind, I thought, *God has placed you in my life for a reason.*

Brian and I said it was a pity there wouldn't be another meeting for a month, but Paula informed us that the medium would be holding one on the upcoming weekend because he had plans and had to move it up. We were delighted and confirmed that we would definitely be there.

We started to pay her for our healings, but she wouldn't accept the money. "This is my gift to you. Remember, you have healing hands."

I couldn't thank her enough for such kindness. What a star she was. "Thank you, Paula. You have helped me so much," I said.

As I made my way to the car, I looked back and saw her standing at the door surrounded by a beautiful prism of light. I thought, *I have seen this light before.*

I knew I wanted to go for another healing. I had experienced a deep awakening. I knew that one day I was going to work with people like Paula. It was like God's universe was presenting to me the things I needed to see in order to find myself and my path.

Brian and I both felt great. I spoke to him about Kim on the way home. I didn't know what to do. Even though our relationship was over, we had not verbalized as much. I really wanted to say I was sorry. I had never meant to hurt her.

I felt like I had found the one true place of happiness, the place I wanted to settle. I loved being around Brian and Tammy; they were such great people. I thought about looking for an apartment. However, there were still obstacles to overcome. I was still an illegal alien, so that meant I couldn't drive, which was a big challenge. It meant if anyone back in Ireland got sick or married, I couldn't go home because I wouldn't be able to get back into America.

I really felt this was my home. I loved the people. I loved the country, with so much choice. I also loved the weather. Experiencing four proper seasons was amazing.

I asked Brian for advice—he always had the right answers! He thought I should phone Kim again and try to make things right, saying it would help me grow. He also said I could stay with them for as long as I wanted to and that there was no rush to get my own place. I knew he meant this from the heart, but I still felt I needed to maybe give them some space. So I planned to stay in America illegally, hoping something would come up that would give me the opportunity to become legal.

Stay or Go? Boom or Bust?

Christmas was around the corner, and I was planning to stay. Brian's business was a little slower than normal. I knew he was under a little pressure, but he didn't tell me much. Things were tight financially. He talked about the boom that was happening back in Ireland, the Celtic tiger, as it was known. It appeared the whole country was working. There were lots of big jobs.

Brian went on to tell me about his reading. The message my grandfather had brought him was that he would go back to Ireland. He didn't think this was going to happen, nor did I. There was too much here for him to pack up and go home to Ireland. He had been in the States for twenty years. I felt that his telling me this was his way of getting some stress off his chest. I didn't think for one minute that he was really considering going home.

Brian was selling some cars at the time. A friend of his came in and fixed them up. He said he was a mechanic, but there is no way he was, because anything he seemed to fix would only get to the front gate of my uncle's place before it broke down. He cost Brian more money and put him under a lot of pressure. My uncle was a kind person, a good Samaritan. He knew this guy needed the money, so he helped him out, but the consequence was that his own pocket was getting emptier.

This was the first time I saw my uncle stressed. I worried about him. I was also thinking a lot about myself and my own future. I didn't want to go back home to Ireland. I didn't know how I would cope.

Would I be back to the partying? Would I walk in those old shoes again? Would I get away from the person everyone feels they know? I am not the guy who got on the plane to come here. If I have to go back, will it still be the same people doing the same things, drinking in bars and telling the same old stories?

Things definitely got me thinking.

18

Validation and Synchronicities at Their Best

On the morning of the next meeting at the medium's, we were all excited. Tammy had arranged a babysitter so all three of us could go. I felt giddy as we waited for the babysitter to arrive. She was running late, and I started to think she wasn't coming.

I asked Brian to give her a call as we didn't want to be late. He tried to ring her but got no answer. He tried again—still no answer. Time was ticking by. Brian said to go ahead and that he would follow when the babysitter arrived.

We all stood in the house, each one of us saying, "No, you go. I will stay." Because I couldn't drive, Brian told me and Tammy to go ahead. I asked the universe to get us there on time. I had my coin and my photos with me, but the only people who knew about that were Brian and Tammy.

We arrived. The place was packed. I took off my shoes on the porch and noticed a change in the weather—it had gotten dull. I saw Paula and a few other faces from the last time as I headed toward the back of the room, to nearly the same seat that I had sat in the first time. I sat beside a pretty woman with blond hair and a soft energy. I was there this time with an open mind, viewing the experience from a whole different place. I felt great.

We waited for the medium to come out and start. I decided to take the coin out of my pocket and hold it in my left hand; the woman was sitting on my right. I gripped it tightly, not letting anyone see it. I looked around the room, sensing the different energies from different people but not seeing any light around them. There was a silence in the room. As the clouds outside changed, so did the light in the room.

The medium appeared and began the class with a different meditation this time. I felt relaxed and felt some sort of connection to the woman sitting next to me, but I was unsure what it was. When the meditation was completed, I felt clear in my mind, at ease. The medium talked about some planetary stuff and things that were shifting, prompting some people to raise their hands and ask questions.

I was still holding my coin out of sight. I could feel my special connection to it. The medium answered people's questions as he made his way around the room. Then he came to the back of the room and stood right in front of me. He looked at me strangely. I was sweating, and my hands felt clammy. I was shaking a little and felt my body temperature change.

"You met her, didn't you?" he said to me. I looked at him, nodding my head.

He said it again. "You met her. You met your guardian angel. She came to you, didn't she?"

"Yes." I nodded. I was filled with excitement and shock. *Oh, my God, he knows! I am getting the biggest validation ever!* Everyone in the room looked at me, and my face turned bright red.

"She gave you something, didn't she? Open your hand, please," he said. I opened my hand, and his face lit up. A glow came from him. "Your guardian angel came to you with this coin as a sign from God. May I hold it, please?" he asked.

"Of course," I replied.

What I remember most was the silence in the room. He took the coin and lifted it up, turning it around so everyone else in the room could see it. He continued, "If I was to put every single person in this room together as one, you would not have as much faith as this young man."

I have to be honest—when I heard this, I sat back in my chair and looked over my shoulder, thinking, *He must be talking about someone else. That's not me!* But that was my insecurity talking.

"You met your guardian angel," he continued. "She gave you your coin of hope and faith."

I was taken aback and still blushing, yet I had the biggest smile on my face. It was all part of the transformation.

He gave me back the coin and said, "You must keep that coin close to you at all times." And then off he went to the next person.

The woman sitting next to me asked if she could see the coin and hold it. I asked her name, and she said it was

Sue-Ellen. I introduced myself and gave her my coin. As she held it, she told me that she had dreamed about me the night before and had seen my coin in the dream. After she woke up, she felt like she had to write it down. "I have it here."

I couldn't believe it! *Holy Moly! What's going on? It seems to be one thing after another. Yet another synchronicity—showing me my life has meaning and depth.*

Sue-Ellen handed me what she had written.

> A cross in his palm, his hands so strong. The cross reminds me of the crosses I bear. It is his faith, his luck? I want to touch it.
>
> Will I feel the strength from it that he does? I want to touch his hand.
> He holds it so tight in his fist. This tells me he believes in it.
> He believes in having something to hold and believes his special gift, his coin.

You can imagine how I was feeling after reading this and hearing the medium validate the visit from my guardian angel and my special coin from God.

> *Life has a plan, and it's our choice to be*
> *awake or asleep along the path.*
> *Thy will, not their will.*

The circle wrapped up for the afternoon. Tammy and I chatted, still in total amazement. She was so supportive, and I was happy that she had been there for the experience. Brian had never made it, though, because the babysitter didn't show. I really wished he had been there. I couldn't wait to tell him what had happened.

Tammy and I each talked to different people, and I turned to see Paula. I was delighted to see her. Some people wanted to see the coin, the start of a long procession of people seeing and holding the special coin. I told Paula a little about how I had received it, and we arranged to meet again, this time at Brian and Tammy's.

I got an opportunity to show the medium my photos, and he confirmed what I had felt. This was more validation. Everything on my path was all falling in place.

It was nearly time for Tammy and me to go home. I exchanged numbers with Sue-Ellen, and we agreed to keep in touch. I was so grateful and was still thinking about her dream and its meaning.

The will of God moves the world.

I didn't stop talking the whole way home. It was lovely to spend some time with Tammy. She had a great sense of humor and a way of bringing out the funny side in me. So the whole way home, she cracked jokes and did silly things. My sides practically needed stitching up afterward because I had laughed so much.

When the medium gave me the validation about my guardian angel, the feelings that ran through my body were euphoric. *What is life showing me at this time?* I was learning that I can have these euphoric moments and be in a place of complete bliss, high on life, without any external influence or substance. I learned that it can all come from within, and this is not something that is just gifted to one person. It is there for us all!

We arrived back at the house buzzing—high on life! Brian, however, was a little quieter than usual. I knew he had really wanted to be there and felt bad that he had missed out. I told him about Sue-Ellen and her dream about me and my coin. I didn't want to go on too much, as I knew he was a little pissed off that the babysitter hadn't shown up.

I met up with Sue-Ellen a couple of times. She was also young and on her own spiritual journey, so we had lots in common. It was great to talk about angels, healing, life, and life experiences. I learned a lot from her. Like me, she had her own spiritual perils along the road to her awakening.

You Better Get Home Quick.
What Goes Up Surely Must Come Down!

One day as Christmas neared, I was helping my uncle in his garage. We had to go to the army barracks to drop off some starters and alternators for some army vehicles he was working on.

Brian had taken in a Ford F350 pickup truck for service with a few other little jobs. He got his buddy the mechanic to do the work.

Now let me explain. Brian's home had a fully working garage that was connected to his home, so we could walk from the house into a little office and straight onto the garage floor. It had a four-poster lift big enough to fit a limousine on. Because it was automated, we could raise a vehicle safely from the ground using just a button. It had a safety mechanism so that, at each level, safety pins would click into place. I had to listen for them. Once I heard all four clicks, I knew it was safe to let the car back down.

We left to make this delivery, and the weather was horrible. It looked like the sky was about to fall out of the heavens. As we drove to the army barracks, Brian noticed he was low on fuel, so we started looking for a gas station.

Before we left, Brian had warned the mechanic to be careful with the lift as the pickup truck was big and heavy. This guy had a habit of half-doing things. Brian's phone rang a couple of times, but he was under a lot pressure to get the job to the army barracks, so he never answered it. We came across a gas station, filled up the tank, and got to the barracks just in the nick of time.

Brian told me that he had a really bad feeling that something was not right. With that, the phone rang again. It was Tammy. There had been an accident back at home. We raced back right away.

We arrived at the house and drove around to the back. The garage door was fully open. I saw the mechanic standing there, as white as a sheet and smoking a cigarette like it was the last one he would ever smoke!

For a split second, we thought Tammy had been messing with us. Then we pulled into full view and saw that the pickup truck had run off the lift, through the wall, and into the office! Brian was completely silent. I had never seen a man so quiet in my life.

The mechanic raced over to the window saying, "I am sorry. I don't know what happened."

In a calm voice, Brian said, "Are you okay?" as he looked at the big pickup truck smashed through the wall of the house. "What happened?"

"I had the lift up full and went to put it down. Three pins stayed locked and the front gave way."

Brian and I knew this wasn't true. He had put the lift up fully but never listened for the four pins locking, so when he had let the lift down again, the pickup went crashing to the ground. What was even scarier was that the kids would often come from the house to the garage if we were there. In fact, Tammy confirmed that the kids had been out there only two minutes before it happened. They were so lucky. Tammy said she had been out by the lift but had a strong urge to go inside with the kids. When she went inside, she heard the crash. I knew that this was God helping.

Brian was still silent apart from making sure everyone was okay. He asked me to make sure everything was switched off and the doors were locked. He said he would be in in a minute. He paid the mechanic, sent him on his way, turned off the rest of the lights, and went into the house.

Everyone was safe. There was nothing we could do about the vehicle in his office. It was all serious, yet I really felt like laughing. Have you ever been in a situation where you really don't want to laugh but you can't help it?

Brian came in, turned the TV on, and didn't say a word. I couldn't look at him because I thought I was going to laugh. Tammy couldn't look at me because she was doing the same—holding in the laughter. All was silent when, out of nowhere, Brian let out a massive scream! He was going mad, screaming his head off. This just completely set me off laughing.

"There is a three-and-a-half-ton pickup in my f---ing office that belongs to a f---ing customer!" he screamed.

I couldn't help but laugh. Tammy started laughing too, then the kids joined in, and before we knew it, we were all laughing. If anyone had seen us, they would have thought we were crazy. From pain to laughter!

At breakfast the next morning, Brian said he was seriously thinking of moving back home. There was so much work in Ireland at that time. I knew his business was sinking him, so it was the best decision for him and his family. But it totally turned my plans upside down. I didn't know what to do; I was in limbo. I needed to make a decision, and I didn't have long to make it.

Brian told me I could stay and live with Tammy's parents. It was a great offer, but my heart said no. Still, I was fearful about going home. Would people understand me now? I was on a spiritual path, not smoking or drinking. I felt that lots of closed minds and big challenges waited for me at home.

Christmas arrived, and we were all in high spirits. Brian and Tammy were excited about their new life in Ireland, and I was just living in the moment. I tried to call Kim over the Christmas holidays, but we never got to speak. I still wanted to make peace after everything she had helped me with. I also wanted to tell her that I was going back home to Ireland.

I started to think about what my life would be like back in Ireland. I called Neala to tell her the news. She asked me to come back to New York, saying that she would find me some work and that I could move back in with her. I just couldn't do it. I didn't feel I was strong enough to live or work in the city. I still had pain from the accident on the Fourth of July. Living with Brian and Tammy had brought me safety, but I would be watching over my shoulder if I moved back to the city. I just couldn't do it. Neala totally understood and wished me well.

It was time to let the others at home know that my American dream was coming to an end. I would probably have to move back in with my parents at first. This would be tough, but I wouldn't stay for long. I called home to tell my family the good news: I would be coming home at the end of January 2003.

I spoke with Mom and I asked her if I could move back in with her and Dad when I came home. She was happy and asked if I would be home in time for Vicky's twenty-first birthday but said that I could surprise her. I was excited about this and was looking forward to seeing her. I was also excited about seeing my little brother, Jason, who I knew wasn't so little anymore. It sounded like he had grown up overnight. I wanted to see my whole family. But would my family know me? I was not the person who had left Ireland back in 2001.

I also asked Mom about my best friend and how he was doing. She said he was not too good. He had been in some trouble, and she didn't think things were going well. I was worried about him.

I wrote often at this point, asking God for guidance. *Why am I going back to Ireland when my heart belongs in America?* I wasn't sure why I felt my heart belonged in America, but the answer for this would come years later.

I carried on many conversations in my mind. I didn't always get a direct answer, but the presence was always there. I still believe it was the never-ending conversations that made me stronger.

We passed through Christmas and into the New Year. January arrived, and the clock was ticking. Brian and Tammy had lots to do. They were selling their belongings and packing up stuff. I wasn't working at the time and didn't have much cash, so they kindly paid for my ticket home.

I was nervous about flying home. *What if I get stopped leaving the country and pulled in for being illegal?* It would be a five- or ten-year ban if I got caught. Would I ever be able to come back?

19

A Visitor with a Difference

B rian and Tammy very rarely relaxed in bed after they woke up, but when they did I went in and chatted to them in their bedroom. Our conversations were always about God, angels, and spirits, and I enjoyed sharing our views.

We were chatting one morning about different things, mostly about going back home to Ireland. It was hard for them. It was such a big move to find new jobs, schools for the kids, and a new home.

They had a small TV in their bedroom that was on in the background as we talked. I was lying at the bottom of their bed when the TV switched off. We didn't pay any attention to it and continued chatting. Then it came back on and went off again.

"Okay, stop messing. Who has the remote control?" Brian asked. I looked at Tammy because she is the joker.

Brian also looked at her. "You have it, don't you, Tammy?"

"No, I haven't," she replied.

"You have them, Robbie?"

"No, I don't," I replied. The TV was back on now. "Come on, you have them!" Tammy and I said to Brian.

"No, I haven't!" he exclaimed.

We started laughing. Tammy looked around and noticed the remote control sitting at the side of the TV. "Look, it's over there," she said, pointing. We all looked at one another, our faces alight.

Brian said, "If there is someone else from the spirit world in this room, then turn the volume up." He no more had the words out when the TV went up to full volume. It was so loud. Brian then asked for the volume to go down, and sure enough, it started to go down. We looked at one another in amazement. The hairs were standing on the backs of our neck and arms!

We still wondered if there was another remote, knowing that there wasn't. We all put our hands out where they were in full view.

"Turn to channel five," Brian said, and the TV switched over to channel five. "Turn to channel thirteen." The TV did as it was asked.

This was some experience. I have had lots of different experiences over the years, but this was one that we were all sharing together.

I felt the energy shift in the room. I felt spirit energy right at the bottom of the bed. Brian decided to ask some different questions. He said to Tammy and me, "It's my dad. It's Paddy."

Tammy and I felt the same.

Brian asked, "Is this you, Dad? If so, turn the TV off."

Nothing happened for a few seconds, then the TV switched off. The three of us nearly fell out of the bed! *Granddad, it's you! Thanks so much for coming today.*

We were all excited. Brian asked, "Is this really you, Dad? If so, turn the TV on and switch to channel six."

There was another pause, and then the TV switched on and changed to channel one, then two, three, four, five, and six, where it stopped.

"It's you, Dad! Thanks so much for coming and letting us all know you are around us."

Tammy and Brian welled up a little, as did I. *We love you so much and miss you so much.* We sat there for the next few minutes without speaking a word.

I thought of Danny. *Can you hear me, Danny?*

The response I got was, "Yes."

Can you tell my Granddad I love him?

"You can tell him."

I love you, Granddad. We love you.

I heard softly in my mind, *I know. I am with you all the time.*

I was so happy.

Brian then said, "I have one more question. Is it a good move for us to go back to Ireland? If so, go back to channel three." Without hesitation, the TV went straight to channel three. That was the confirmation Brian needed. It helped put away a lot of doubt. The TV switched off, the room heated up again, and they were gone.

We all had some excitement that day. The happiness I felt for my uncle Brian was immense. I was thrilled that

Granddad had come and given Brian a sign that it was okay to move to Ireland and that things would work out.

Sue-Ellen and I had plans together. She worked in a hair salon and was going to give me a haircut, and then we were going to spend the day hanging out. I didn't have much time left in the States and wanted to spend as much time with her and Paula before I left, as the three of us had such a great connection.

I started to think that I didn't want to go back to Ireland, so I confided in Sue-Ellen about this. She suggested that I could stay with her instead. I really considered it—I felt so torn. Everything was okay when I had the support of Brian and Tammy, but would I survive after they left? Sue-Ellen was so generous, and in some sense she was saying, "I will look after you."

I spoke to her about my not being able to drive and said that it was a lot harder to get work outside of the city. She understood but probably wasn't thinking things through fully. It simply wouldn't be realistic to stay.

At this time, Sue-Ellen was going through a lot of stuff herself and was only now getting her life back on track. We agreed that going home and looking for work would be my best option. That was the plan.

I waited at the salon until she finished her shift, and then we took off for a really cool crystal shop that she had wanted to visit. It was really nice, with lots of crystals and books. I went outside and waited for Sue-Ellen while she was browsing in the shop.

When she came out, she showed me that she had bought a little gift. It was a bookmark that said "Faith" and had a symbol on it. "I got this for you to represent your faith. When you read it, you will see how strong your faith is." I was delighted and thanked her for the perfect gift.

Sue-Ellen dropped me off at home that evening. I looked into her eyes and felt like we had a special connection, a really strong friendship.

After I went to bed that night, I lay there asking my usual questions to God about my life. *Where am I going, and what will I do?* I asked my angel what the true meaning of hope was. *Why have you brought this to me?* I kept saying, "Hope," over and over again. I must have drifted off at some stage because I woke at 3:33 a.m.

"It's Time to Wake Up—Your Answer Has Come!"

I was awakened and tried to bring my eyes into focus while turning my bedside lamp on. I heard the voice in my mind as softly as the first time I had heard it.

"Can you hear me, dear one? Your answer has come. It's time for you to understand the meaning of hope. You have come a long way since you looked for your sign. When it came to you at the garage, the time was perfect for this. We told you that you would doubt and that you would still have times of doubt, but your faith is what would save you. The answers you seek will come, and it will be in divine timing. You are now starting to understand energy and the light again."

"Where are you?" I asked. "Why can't I see you?"

"Turn your lamp off and close your eyes."

I felt the room get really warm. The energy completely changed.

"Open your eyes slowly."

I began to open my eyes, but all I could see was light, clear and bright. I asked, "Why am I seeing you this way?"

"Because this is what we really are! We only appear to each person as they can handle us, or in the way they have been told about us or have imagined us in their minds. When the time is right, we will appear to them as you see me now. I come from the light of God. I can take many shapes and forms. I am showing you so you will recognize me and other angels from now on."

"I have seen this light before," I said.

"Yes, dear one, you have, but so have others. The white light you see is what some people describe as our wings."

"Will I see you or the other angels in any other form?" I asked.

"Yes, I told you we will appear in many shapes and forms. You can see me tonight in my purest essence. You will not have every answer now, but you will grow. And as you grow, your light will grow so others may see you."

"I feel things around people, and my hands get tingly and hot," I replied.

"This light and energy comes from God. This energy you feel is within every single soul. You all have the ability to use and connect to it. Dear one, you chose this journey to help others. It's your wisdom from other lifetimes you will share. You must be a beacon, not only to the light, but also to bring light to the darkness, helping people to see their light. Sometimes it will be the darkness that you see most, but remember: we surround you in love from the great divine. You will help bring light to people's shadows, and on a soul level, they will understand. But in the physical, they will try to hide their pain or disillusions. They may even try to hurt you. We are watching over you and protecting you. Don't fear; just be love and light. Search for the truth, and keep on searching for your teacher, as it is his teachings that you will mostly help people through. The time will come when all will fall into place, but up until then you will feel like you are being left behind fighting many battles. The time will be perfect for you, and this is when you will bring the message of hope to the world."

"What? So I am sharing the message?"

"Yes. God's message is simply love and peace to all. And the true meaning of hope is 'Help Other People Evolve.' Be of good service to others; help those souls to see their light.

"Too many souls are helping themselves and not for the good of humanity; this needs to change so that humanity can change. Help other people recognize their journey and tell them it is a journey of meaning. Help them to see the light that is within. It is very important to recognize the soul that is far worse off than you are—this will teach you compassion and take away the emptiness that is within. Don't cross the street to pass them by if someone should ask you for help. Help them. Give to them from your heart and not the mind—this is love. Don't give to receive. When you come from a place of love, you have already received.

"These are all simple principles that you must live by if you want to fulfill your life and destiny. You must all stand united, hand in hand in peace and love, and there shall not be one mouth that should go unfed. The time of war should come to an end. So you may all evolve, not just a select few—it is not the will of God to leave one soul in the darkness. As I have explained before, we come from a place on high that most humans have yet to understand, but consciousness is changing so others may become aware."

I wanted to know more about the message I was being given. "How do people receive God's message?"

"It's important that you help others understand about living a life that is full of gratitude, helping them to understand the law of attraction. You will also help people to remove negative blockages from their minds, their bodies, and their homes. People will come to you for healing and your advice, and one day you will stand in front of an audience, telling them about these events in your life."

I couldn't see this at the time. Everything was all so new, and this sounded like a mammoth task. I had started to write in a diary, and even this was a challenge! Little did I know that these diaries would one day serve such a purpose.

She reassured me. "Don't be afraid to write. This will become much easier as your mind begins to heal. The reason you struggled so much in school was because you had to choose to keep the right side of the brain more open, and anything that defined logic would have suppressed you even more. So the battle through education was all part of your awakening. You will understand all your lost memories through the practice of meditation and karmic life lessons. The memories that are locked away from your childhood will soon become free—this will become the second part of your story. You have an intelligence that has not come from books. It comes from the very essence of your soul, and it's your journey now to share this with many others. Keep helping others; continue on that path. It's time to stop beating yourself up. A great healing will come your way, and then, through the light of God, you will Help Other People Evolve."

"So I will remember things from my childhood?" I asked.

"Yes. Karma is the key to understanding these blocks and the pain that you suffered throughout your childhood. Do not focus on the blame but on the healing, as everybody has to take responsibility for the actions. As you give it is how you shall receive. Remember, the answers will not come tonight, so be patient. This is not your first lifetime. Trust in God, and your coin will also guide you along the journey. There may be many people who will want to hold your coin, and this can also bring them great healing; instill hope and faith in others. So the answer is, you are just one seed, but from this, many others will grow. If you build it, they will come. Have faith; God has a divine plan for you, and one day you will look back and this won't seem as unreal as it does now. What you will learn will be that the only one true answer in this world will be one of love and peace. Don't be afraid to speak from your heart, as this will guide you to every single word that you need to reach others."

This was really a lot for me to take in at this point, and I was trying to embrace the moment. Just like all of us, I still had a lot to learn.

"Our message for you and each and every other soul is to always go back to your creator—the great I Am presence: God. This will always be the only answer, for it is God's love that you know best. It is God's will for you all to remember that. Your coin will be a symbol of hope—you will be the beacon of light to which it will come.

"I am with you at every moment. Just call me when you are most in need and I will come."

I thanked her again, and with that she was gone. I felt very grateful at this moment. Then I felt the energy shift, and I fell back to sleep straightaway. I slept like a baby.

When I woke the next morning, the first thing I felt was gratitude in my heart. My first thoughts were of the meaning of *hope*—"Help Other People Evolve." The answer was one of service and how best to serve others.

I had the poem "Footprints in the Sand" ringing through my mind, which I had seen every single day as a child and as a young adult. It hung on the wall in my grandmother's bathroom, so I couldn't help but read it every time I went in. I never fully understood it when I was younger, but now I know the true meaning.

God is everything. God is real—so real. I have received more than one validation in my life. God has answered my prayers, helping me to begin to let go of old patterns and thoughts that I once struggled with. The answer I received was that God is and will always be talked about in books and many rules will be made in the name of God, but really, the truth is within us all. There are no rules to what God is; it is no one thing and it is everything. There are no limits and no description on this earth that can describe the source of God and creation.

All creation is energy; everything in creation is energy. Remember that you have a straight connection to the Father, his son Jesus Christ, the Holy Spirit, and when you know this, develop your own understanding, not someone else's interpretation. It is beyond thought; therefore, we will call it all that is, was, and will be. If you continually search for false idols and your search is an external one, you may miss God because God is your feelings, your experience, and everything that you are. God isn't what you believe; it's what you are and what you do.

Knowing is your own experience, and belief is just a system that someone else preaches. Do not tell me, but show me. The limitations of language, time, and space may hinder my explanation, but my soul knows God and your soul knows God. There is a hierarchy of communication between your soul and God.

God's love, to and for us, is untouchable. I began to learn to live my life outside of the dogma of others. It was important for me to learn to read between the lines and not let others control my path with misguided information. And remember also, what I speak about is coming from my own personal experience. It's important for you to learn to discern.

God is and always has been unconditional love, shining forth to the children of this earth. God has not only brought me validations but has sent me my guardian angel. God's love has always been trying to show us something, but the ill will of humankind has caused the separation between

God and us. Beings that come from a fear-based ego are anti-Christ and demonized; they are possessed. When I start to look back at my life, I can see the control of these beings, but even through all of this, God's love has never left me.

Nor will it ever leave you.

Love those who harm you, forgive those who hurt you; give to those who steal from you. Speak from your heart with kindness, compassion, and understanding. We all know these truths.

In the end, what we choose will truly determine whom and what we really are.

20

We Are All One

Brian told me about all the bits and pieces he and Tammy had to take care of before moving back to Ireland. They were planning on flying into Ireland and then back to America to finalize things before returning home for good. I thought I might come back to America myself.

I decided not to tell Brian about my recent message, as I didn't feel it was the right time for me to talk about it. I was processing so much through my heart; I was still learning and growing through my own pain and understanding.

Circle

Paula and Sue-Ellen arrived at Brian and Tammy's for our own little meeting that we had planned. I told Paula about all that had been happening lately, and she said that she thought it would not be long before I would be stepping into my own working shoes. I thanked her again for the healing, as I felt it helped me to open up greatly.

The conversation was wonderful and so open—we all got on so well. Paula started talking about healing and meditation. I really enjoyed listening to her knowledge and wisdom. She brought us through a lovely guided meditation, and we all experienced the energy in the room shifting. It felt like the room was full of beautiful, gentle energy. I would definitely say that this was like my training ground, helping me to understand different experiences.

We all enjoyed the moment. Everyone was feeling this, not just a select one or two, proving that it was there for all of us. What this also showed us was that on our own we are strong, but united we are stronger—we can hold more energy. It was God's way of saying that there is a special key: meditation. And if you show up, the energy will turn up.

Surprise, Surprise!

I had phoned home a couple of times, and we decided that I would surprise everyone for Vicky's twenty-first birthday. I was going to get the chance to see all of my friends and family. I tried to think what they would be like when they saw me.

I wasn't drinking or smoking anymore. I now spent my time writing in a journal, meditating, and browsing through books. My family were in for a shock! I knew they would wonder where the party animal had gone. In America, I was surrounded by so many like-minded people, and I knew that going home to all my friends and family who were not as much into God and the angels would be hard.

What will my life be like back in Ireland? I won't stay for long—I'll go home for a few weeks and then book a flight back.

I'll take my chances in America.

"I Have a Gift for You"

Sue-Ellen came to pick me up, and we went out for some food at a really cool burger joint that held a lot of joy and laughter. The food was great, and the atmosphere was even better. The place contained great energy. We were really enjoying our night, eating well, and chatting about the future.

"I have a gift for you. I got you a little something," Sue-Ellen said. "You can open one, but I don't want you to open the other until you are on the plane home."

One of them was wrapped like it was a book. I chose to unwrap the other present, a little pouch that said "Hope" on the outside. I pulled the strings apart and emptied the contents onto my hand. Out came two beautiful silver angels, one slightly bigger than the other. The biggest one was the Angel of Hope and the other was the Angel of Love. This was the most amazing gift ever!

I felt like crying because of the thought that she had put into the gift. They were perfect for the journey on which I was about to embark. I hugged her and thanked her so much. This was so thoughtful. I had my coin in a cloth, so I took it out and put the three of them together.

From that day until now, they have remained together and have never been separate from one another for a single moment. They have never been separate from me, either; they have been in my pocket every day and have sat by my bed every single night over these years.

We spent the rest of the evening together talking about many things, thanking the universe for igniting our friendship even for the shortest time—only six weeks! She made me promise not to open the other gift until my plane took off. I promised.

The day before I flew home, Brian, Tammy, and I were checking things off our lists. I was feeling a little nervous about getting out of the country. The airline emailed Tammy looking for the number on my holiday visa. It was the number of the waiver visa I had filled in when I came into the country. They take it back off you when you leave. I ripped the piece of paper with the number on it out of my passport based on advice from a friend, who told me that if I got stopped I should say I lost it, and then they wouldn't know how long I had been there for.

Brian told me not to worry, that lots of people would do that, but I think he was only saying this to make me feel better. My thoughts were with God and his angels. I wanted them to guide me through whatever was coming up. I was all packed up and ready to go, but I really wanted to talk to Kim one last time. I wanted to thank her, wish her well, and say goodbye.

I picked up the phone and made the call. It rang and rang. I was about to hang up when Kim finally answered.

"Hello."

I knew by her voice that she didn't really want to speak. "I have to tell you that I am sorry, Kim," I said. "I am really sorry for hurting you. I am leaving tomorrow to go back home to Ireland."

"I knew this would happen, Robbie. I knew this time would come," she said.

"I never planned for it to work out this way; it just happened." I think she knew at this point that it wasn't my plan to hurt her. It wasn't something I had set out to do. I felt she was still hurting, so our conversation was short. I was so sad to hear her hurting, but I had to let go of the pain. And when I did, it felt like a massive weight had been lifted off my shoulders. I wished her well and put down the phone.

It's important to know that everything happens for a reason, and sometimes in life, when we are in the middle of things, we fail to notice this. It doesn't mean that it's not all still happening perfectly. We, and we alone, are the only people driving our ships; no one else will see through your eyes, just like no one else will see the last thing you see before you sleep or the first thing you see when you wake. We have to make choices in this life. Sometimes that can be hurtful or may cause pain and other times it may seem effortless, but choices are always important. Taking responsibility is our biggest lesson, but it will not be our only one.

I spent the day before I was due to leave visiting Tammy's family and some friends I had made to say my farewells. A wise man once told me: you only ever say goodbye to a person if you know you'll *never* see them again—at least in the physical. If for any reason you think you *will* see that person again, it is always better to say, "I will see you later."

I was very grateful for Sue-Ellen's kindness and support, but the time was coming to say goodbye. I was sad at the thought of leaving all my friends, though through my sadness, I was also grateful for my journey in America. It wasn't all bad. I still have so many happy memories there, and I will always love the US of A. What a roller coaster ride it had been.

I had left Ireland lost, going through all my experiences, and when I came to America, I found myself again. I found hope. My faith was now sealed, and my belief was rock solid. Through every single moment, I have been blessed and looked after. My new job would be working for God's universe. The soul had found the soul, thus giving the soul a purpose.

The Next Leg of the Journey

As we approached the airport, I felt nervous and anxious, worried about the possibility of being stopped. We went over to the Aer Lingus check-in desk. Tammy could see I was really anxious. My knees were knocking, and let me tell you, it was very visible. My hands were even rattling! Tammy got me to hold one of the kid's hands as she thought it would relax me, and it did.

At the check-in desk, I had my passport in my hand. My turn was next. A young Irish-American guy was working on the desk. I handed him my passport, and he asked me, "Were you over for long?"

"Just a couple of months," I replied.

He looked at my passport and asked, "Where is your holiday visa waiver?"

Now this was all post-9/11, so things were a lot tighter security-wise. I explained that I had lost my holiday visa waiver, and he gave me a funny look. He looked at the date with the stamp that said I had arrived in 2001. My mind was racing. *Please help me.*

I felt light around us; I knew God and his angels were helping. He looked at my passport again. "There is one of the pages signed. Did you know that?" he asked.

"Yes, a famous singer signed his autograph on my passport on a night out," I replied.

Let me rewind the clock just a tick.

While I was living in Manhattan, I went to a bar called the Red Lion one day with one of my buddies where there was an open-mic session. A friend of mine worked behind the bar. We were drinking away when we noticed a famous singer by the name of Shawn Mullins. He sang that song called "Lullaby." I was a little starstruck, so I bought him a pint and we ended up having a few beers with him! Before he left, I asked him to give me his autograph, but the only thing I had was my passport. He very hesitantly signed it. *Oops, maybe that wasn't such a good idea after all!*

So I was standing at the airport check-in, waiting for the SWAT team to jump me. I may have been slightly paranoid. It really felt like the moment was being overshadowed by

ROBBIE H. ANDREWS

the light, and I kept seeing flashes of ocean-blue light around the ticket agent.

He dropped something on the floor, and when he stood back up, he looked at me, stamped my passport, and said, "Okay, enjoy your flight."

Thank you! Thank you! Thank you!

We boarded the plane. I sat in my seat waiting for the door to close. As we were still on American soil, I didn't feel 100 percent free. It's amazing how the mind can be so irrational when filled with fear. I wasn't a criminal; granted, I had overstayed my welcome, but it was all part of my path, my divine plan, and my soul's agreement.

The captain spoke over the PA system, saying that we were ready to taxi to the runway. The stewards locked the door, and I felt a massive sense of relief. The engines fired up, and we were off. The front wheels left the ground, and I was no longer on American soil. I was about to begin the next leg of my journey.

I remembered that I still had Sue-Ellen's gift to open, so I looked inside the bag and opened it. I thought it was a book, but it wasn't. It was a diary, a beautiful, hardbacked writing book. I opened it and turned to the first page, where there was a handwritten message.

01-23-2003
Dear Robbie,

Some people only worry about getting the best out of life. Few people like you, special

218

people like you, know that it's more important to give life your best.

You're dreaming new dreams, learning new things, and accepting new challenges. Some people are afraid of opening new doors and taking risks, but you are not like that. You're strong, your faith is powerful and will guide you to new levels, higher levels.

Moment by moment, day by day you are becoming the person you want to be. You are someone I admire and someone I am proud to know.

Especially, you're someone that I believe in and someone who has taught me a lot about love, faith and how to cherish life.

Thank you for all that you have given me. I'll meet you there.

Love,
Sue-Ellen xx

To Be Continued

I would like to share this beautiful poem that was given to me by a very dear friend. It is about my journey and coin.

Heartfelt gratitude to you, Sandra. Thank you.

The Sign

As I sat with great interest and listened to your story, How you struggled to cope at the start of your journey. That you had hit rock bottom to see the light ahead, You then took the right path and here is where it's led.

You asked God, "If this is real then give me a sign."
And your Guardian Angel appeared and gave you your special coin.
You communicated daily with the Angels, Spirits and Guides, And I wouldn't say its easy work but you take it in your stride.

You're spiritually gifted Robbie and you've already helped so many. God and the Angels knew this and sent your special penny.

Prayer and Invocation

Jesus, our Light & Savior.

Lord Jesus the Christ, thank you for bringing me here.

Lord Jesus, I open my heart today. I invite you to come inside.

Come O Lord, and save my life; receive me today as a child of God.

Forgive all my sins and write my name in the Book of Life.

I give myself to you: my spirit, my soul, my body.

Receive me O Lord Jesus the Christ.

Now, devil.

The blood of Jesus is against you. I command you now, to leave me. I don't belong to you.

I am God's property.

Leave my life. I disassociate myself from you.

I renounce every evil covenant I have entered in with you.

In Jesus name, I have received salvation.

I am a child God.

Amen.

This prayer and invocation I shared with you is very blessed. It will protect you and help you to end all curses that have been cast upon you and your family for generations. Please use this daily and as much as you need. Share this with your family and friends and as many people as you know. Watch God's plan unfold in your life and remember his love for you.

I would like to say a very special thank you to Buddha Maitreya, the reincarnation of Jesus the Christ, for all your help and every single thing you do for humanity.

Blessings to you all,
The Angel Man.

About the Author

Hi, friends! This is the part where I get to tell you a little bit about myself—what I do and why I do it. One thing that strikes me right through to my core is that I've always had this burning desire to help people, to be of service to people. Helping people is what I do.

I'm a healer, meditator and life mentor. I've spent the vast majority of my time since 2003 aiding people in their troubles and bringing the light to the darkness. I mostly do this on a one-to-one basis but also offer group sessions, and I work with clients who come from far and wide to experience my healing services. In these, I use various methods. My empathic nature helps people to heal and move toward a more positive path. I have a good success rate when it comes to helping others to heal, and there's a simple reason behind that: It's what I came here to do.

Here's a list of *some* of the reasons people come to me:

- Feeling stuck or drained or procrastinating
- Finding it hard to remove toxic, negative patterns
- Feeling low or depressed

- Feeling negative psychic attacks
- Experiencing bad energy in their homes
- Experiencing emptiness
- Having troubles in workplace or business premises

If any of the things on this list or things similar to them are problems that you are dealing with, you can visit my website and view all the details on how to book an appointment there:

www.robbiehandrews.com

Printed in the United States
By Bookmasters